THE COFFEE BOOK

JACKI BAXTER

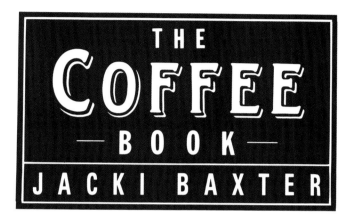

THE COFFEE BOOK

JACKI BAXTER

Eagle
Editions

A QUANTUM BOOK

Published by Eagle Editions
an imprint of Eagle Remainders Ltd
2A Kingsway, Royston
Hertfordshire SG8 5EG

ISBN 1-902328-30-2

QUMCOF

This book is produced by
Quantum Books Ltd
6 Blundell Street
London N7 9BH

Art Director Peter Bridgewater
Editor Polly Powell
Photographers Trevor Wood and Mike Bull
Illustrator Lorraine Harrison
Home Economists Felicity Jeliff and
Brenda Smith

Printed in Dubai by Oriental Press

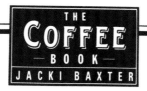

Contents

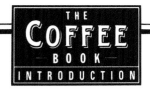
Beyond the Bean

"COFFEE SHOULD BE BLACK AS HELL, STRONG AS DEATH, AND SWEET AS LOVE" *Turkish proverb.*

In an age of instant coffee, coffee bags, or vacuum-packed 'real' coffee sold in super-markets and hypermarkets, the traditional coffee retailer is something of an oddity, a throwback. In some ways it is surprising that it still exists, but it does and what is more it seems to be thriving! My favourite one has a traditional wooden frontage painted dark brown with the proprietor's name picked out in antique yellow gold above the window in which are arranged various packeted brands of tea, cookies and other specialist delicacies. There is an ancient, but cheerfully striped awning which is lowered on warm sunny days to protect the window display. Situated in the left side of the window is an antiquated coffee roaster with a metal perforated drum. At the top of the window is a vent, out of which the delicious aromatic smoke of roasting coffee beans billows forth to waft onto the busy street. Of course, the marvellous aroma of coffee attracts people in a steady stream throughout the day. If it were not for this busy atmosphere you might think you were in a museum, for everything down to the brown paper bags and old-fashioned till is just as it would have been eighty years ago.

Inside, it is darkly painted. At the end is a little hatch where the cashier sits. Underfoot are bare wooden floorboards. The left hand wall is lined with shelves laden with numerous packets, jars and tins of edible delights. On the floor propped against the left-hand wall are sacks of green coffee beans, mainly blends; Kenyan, Algerian, Continental, Jamaican Blue Mountain, Mocha and more! To the right, running the length of the room is a traditional, solid, wooden mahogany counter upon which rest old-fashioned scales. Behind the counter, the walls are lined with shelves carrying an array of paper packets containing various blends of pre-roasted coffee beans.

The owner and his family run the business and are connoisseurs; they are quite happy to stand and discuss blends and roasting techniques for as long as the customer wishes. Why has this specialist survived when so many have long since disappeared? The answer lies partly in the skilful management of the family who own it but more likely because of the enduring and now increasing popularity of real coffee blended and roasted according to the traditional time-honoured way. One hundred years ago specialist coffee retailers like this one proliferated in every village, town and city in the civilized world and the homely routine of roasting and grinding coffee beans was part of the rhythm of everyday life.

For coffee is the world's favourite beverage and is enjoyed the world over in many different forms. There is nothing more homely and reassuring than the sound of coffee brewing on the hearth as the delectable aroma fills the parlour. The offer of a cup of coffee today is more than an offer of a drink; it is a gesture of friendship.

However, throughout its long and eventful history the humble coffee bean has been loved and hated, condemned as Satan's brew, the subject of prohibition to the common folk, blessed by a Pope, smuggled across oceans, protected by armed guards, and these are but a few of the myths and legends that surround it. All this drama lies behind the cup of coffee which you sip each morning blissfully unaware!

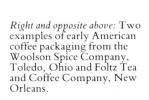

Right and opposite above: Two examples of early American coffee packaging from the Woolson Spice Company, Toledo, Ohio and Foltz Tea and Coffee Company, New Orleans.

Beyond the Be...

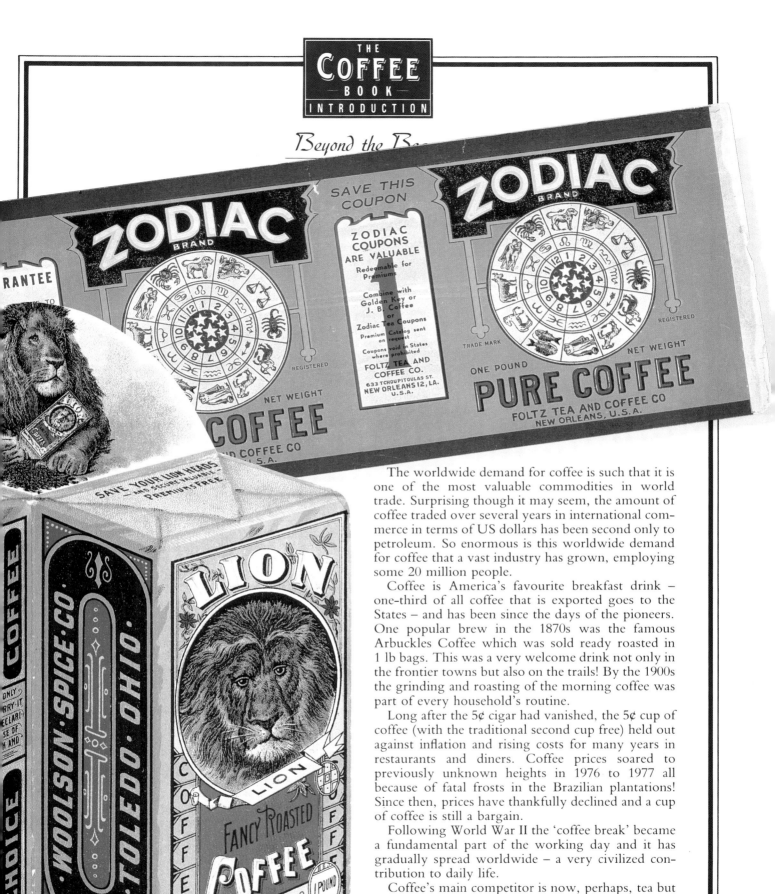

The worldwide demand for coffee is such that it is one of the most valuable commodities in world trade. Surprising though it may seem, the amount of coffee traded over several years in international commerce in terms of US dollars has been second only to petroleum. So enormous is this worldwide demand for coffee that a vast industry has grown, employing some 20 million people.

Coffee is America's favourite breakfast drink – one-third of all coffee that is exported goes to the States – and has been since the days of the pioneers. One popular brew in the 1870s was the famous Arbuckles Coffee which was sold ready roasted in 1 lb bags. This was a very welcome drink not only in the frontier towns but also on the trails! By the 1900s the grinding and roasting of the morning coffee was part of every household's routine.

Long after the 5¢ cigar had vanished, the 5¢ cup of coffee (with the traditional second cup free) held out against inflation and rising costs for many years in restaurants and diners. Coffee prices soared to previously unknown heights in 1976 to 1977 all because of fatal frosts in the Brazilian plantations! Since then, prices have thankfully declined and a cup of coffee is still a bargain.

Following World War II the 'coffee break' became a fundamental part of the working day and it has gradually spread worldwide – a very civilized contribution to daily life.

Coffee's main competitor is now, perhaps, tea but at the height of its popularity in the UK in the 17th century, when coffee houses abounded, it was far

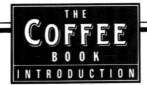

Beyond the Bean

more popular. Again in the 1950s there was a fragile and short-lived mini-boom with the spread of coffee bars which unfortunately quickly plummeted to the depths of obscurity. Tea drinking had a strong grip on the English during World War II. They could not obtain sufficient tea and were forced to drink coffee essences. Even so, coffee was not particularly liked as is revealed by the fact that it was not considered important enough to be rationed. In 1944, when the Americans requested British supplies to help feed Europe after the liberation, the amount of coffee they requested exceeded Britain's entire stocks at the time!

Back in the 17th century, coffee houses were then the refuge of men of business who gathered to discuss their affairs. Eventually they transformed themselves into private businesses – Lloyds, which today insures everything from ships to American spacecraft, had its humble origins in Edward Lloyd's coffee house which opened in London in 1668. The long hours their menfolk spent in the coffee houses so incensed the women of the day that they organized a deputation against these vile establishments on the grounds that coffee made their men 'unfruitful'. This is not the only story of disagreements between the sexes involving coffee! In Turkey, in times gone by, a wife had legitimate grounds for divorce if her husband failed to supply her daily quota of coffee every day of their married life. However, it is not all war between the sexes where coffee is concerned. Nowadays many a romance has begun after an invitation 'to come in for coffee' at the end of an enjoyable evening.

Of course, coffee is renowned for its potency as a stimulant as well as for its delicious flavour. Thousands of students all over the world can confirm its powers. This singular attribute has also been noted by well-known authors throughout history. Emile Zola was one such author who was particularly enamoured with the power of coffee to stimulate his creative work without causing any untoward side effects. However, coffee's powers of stimulation have been cause for concern throughout the centuries. Indeed, Voltaire's physicians were very keen to tell him of the harm that came from the abuse of coffee, claiming that it acted as a poison. Unperturbed, Voltaire calmly answered that it must be a slow poison because if it was so he had been poisoning himself for almost eighty years!

Many people, perhaps not sharing Voltaire's opinion, who fear or suffer from the effects of caffeine (the stimulant in coffee) prefer to drink decaffeinated coffee which, although it lacks the taste

THE LONDON COFFEE-STALL.
[From a Daguerreotype by BEARD.]

of real coffee, is better than drinking no coffee at all!

As one of the world's largest growers of coffee, Brazil's economy relies heavily on coffee. Needless to say, Brazilians love coffee for its taste too. The bustling streets of Rio are filled with coffee carriers delivering the brew to thirsty office workers and it is not exceptional for up to 20 cups per day to be drunk per person! The morning brew is likely to be *café au lait* which is half coffee, half milk and a good spoonful of sugar. Later in the day the brew changes to *caffezinho* which is only for those with an exceptionally sweet tooth – the cups are almost filled with brown sugar and the black coffee is poured over it!

Music and coffee have been linked throughout the centuries. Bach was moved to compose his well-known 'Coffee Cantata' not only to praise the drink but also in order to lampoon (with the aid of

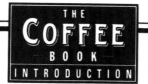

Beyond the Bean

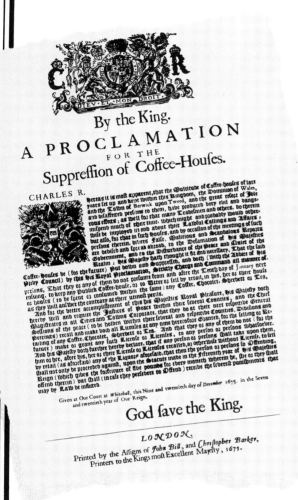

roasted and brewed by boiling with plenty of sugar and concentrated milk served in little glasses. The Bedouins in Libya cook their breakfast coffee out in the sandy desert on a glowing fire in a brazier. They serve the surprisingly weak brew in handleless porcelain cups, shaped like over-sized thimbles. The Italians have little porcelain cups with handles for their famous *espresso* brew and larger, fuller cups for the frothy delight known as *cappuccino*. So varied and so attractive are the many coffee containers around the world that some connoisseurs have been prompted to start collecting them.

What are your favourites? Which coffee is best for which occasion? It's all a matter of taste really. More and more specialist retailers are opening and supermarkets and hypermarkets are increasingly stocking greater varieties of coffee. In most large stores you can find innumerable varieties of coffee including blends of coffee beans; different grinds for different brewings and even in some stores, vacuum-packed beans. Be adventurous and try as many different types of blends and roast as you can before settling on your favourite. You are now entering the realms of connoisseur coffee drinking and your specialist storekeeper will be delighted to help you! You might even be tempted to progress to roasting your own beans or even blending them at home.

If all this sounds beyond your wit, do not despair because this book is designed to help you and to introduce you to the world of real coffee. You are now ready to experience the world beyond the bean!

Picander, a popular satirist) a German movement whose object was to prevent women consuming coffee on the grounds that it made them sterile! Beethoven was also kindly disposed towards coffee and although he composed no special work to immortalize it, he took special care over his coffee drinking. He is reputed to have laboriously counted out sixty coffee beans for every cup of coffee he consumed, so that each cup would be of uniform strength! Bob Dylan's 'One more cup of coffee for the road' suggests that 20th-century composers are no less enthusiastic about coffee than Bach.

Just as wonderful as the varieties of coffee are the various different containers used for serving it. The Belgians favour large plain bowls (which can hold up to two normal size cups) for their early morning *café au lait*. In Laos, they prefer their thick coffee dark

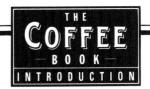
Coffee Around the World

F JULES VERNE's hero, Phineas Fogg, had taken coffee with his breakfast on each day of his 80-day journey, incredibly he would still only have sampled a small proportion of the enormous variety of blends that can be found around the world. For all we know he probably did and would have discovered as many different ways of brewing coffee as the many and varied regions through which he travelled. Naturally, wherever you go people believe that their way of making and serving coffee is the definitive method. In the countries that follow, you can compare the national characteristics and habits, and form your own conclusions.

HOLLAND/KOFFIE

Being astute traders, the Dutch realized early on the commercial potential of the coffee bean, and the 17th century found them cultivating coffee in Java and selling the beans to Europe. This strong connection with the coffee trade meant that the Dutch soon learned to appreciate the delightful taste of the golden brown bean as well as its financial value. Consequently, coffee houses sprang up in Dutch towns and cities, and this tradition continues today as visitors to Holland will confirm.

The bean favoured by the Dutch is carefully roasted to a full medium strength and customarily gently brewed by the Drip method (see page 34). When ordering coffee you are certain to receive a tray on which is placed an individual pot of coffee, a small jug of cream, some sugar and a glass of water – everything you could require, whatever your taste, and a charming touch which never fails to impress the weary tourist.

GREECE/KAFES
TURKEY/KAVÉ

Their thick, syrupy coffee is made by the *ibrik* method (see page 37) and is steeped in ancient customs. According to these rituals, the coffee must be boiled three times before serving. Moreover, it is the custom to serve the oldest and most respected member of the gathering first, and, as a full cup shows dislike of the person to whom it is offered, the small cups are only half filled. A note of warning: allow the coffee to settle before drinking if you wish to avoid a mouthful of grounds.

FRANCE/CAFÉ

Who could imagine France without coffee? They even named bars after their favourite beverage. Drinking a bowl of *café au lait* into which warm freshly baked croissants are dipped is an early morning ritual for the French. Later in the morning they may be seen drinking demitasse cups of strong black coffee. In rural areas this mid-morning coffee is often accompanied by an alcoholic nip!

Most of the coffee served in France is pure and the distinctive bitter taste is due to the very high roast preferred by the French. Chicory is often added but only as an economy measure. The majority of French coffee is brewed by the drip or filter method; coffee correctly brewed in this way is constantly clear and aromatic.

ITALY/CAFFÉ

Italy is a land of dedicated coffee drinkers. In the morning you can find them sipping *caffé latte* from large cups. *Caffé latte* is a high roast *espresso* coffee produced by brewing and mixing a ¼ coffee and ¾

Coffee around the World

hot milk. After both lunch and dinner, the Italians sample the delights of the classic *espresso* brew. This is served in demitasse cups often accompanied by a twist of lemon peel either in the coffee or curled around the rim of the cup.

In between times there is yet another choice! Of course, this is *cappuccino*, so-called because of its similarity in colour to the robes of the Capuchin monks. *Cappuccino* is *espresso* coffee blended with hot frothy milk which has been forced from a syphon under pressure, and sometimes whipped cream is added. Whichever way the drink is served, it is topped with sprinkled cinnamon or cocoa. If you have a taste for variety in your coffee drinking then Italy is the place for you. Try *espresso* served with iced water in one of the innumerable bars of Italy's picturesque towns and cities. Viva Italia!

MOROCCO/QAHWA

Qahwa is made in the Turkish style (see page 37); thick, strong and sweet. Moroccan coffee drinkers often add fiery peppercorns and salt to increase the flavour of the coffee. Admittedly this is an acquired taste but one well worth attempting.

INDIA/COFFEE

Although we tend to think of India as a tea drinking nation it is, in fact, a country divided in its drinking habits; generally, the North drinks tea and the South drinks coffee. The coffee brewed in the South is made by roasting the beans which are then finely

Above left: A typical café scene with customers watching the world go by while drinking their cups of coffee.
Above right: This mobile coffee-making machine from North Africa brews a form of Turkish coffee.
Opposite above: The French name many of their bars after their favourite (non-alcoholic!) beverage.

ground, mixed with raw palm sugar and water, and then heated until cooked. Finally, milk is added and the coffee is ready.

Coffee is served throughout the day, either on its own, or to complement the wide variety of hot vegetarian dishes served in the South. The main meal of the day in southern India is lunch which is invariably followed by coffee. What is usually known as tea-time in other parts of the world is called coffee-time in this region, and drinks are served accompanied by a delicious variety of savoury snacks made from all kinds of pulses (legumes), herbs and spices.

SOVIET UNION/KOFÉ

The Russians are relatively recent converts to coffee and in their country the samovar still rules. They drink their coffee in the same way as their tea – that is, with a slice of lemon.

FINLAND/KAHVI

The Finnish have the reputation of being the largest consumers of coffee in the world. Five cups of coffee

Coffee Around the World

JAPAN/KOOHII

Japan is the largest importer of Jamaican Blue Mountain which according to some experts is the best coffee in the world. Although a cup of coffee in a Japanese coffee house might be considered expensive by some, rest assured it is an unforgettable taste. In their lively, bustling cafés the Japanese drink all types of coffee including *espresso, cappuccino,* iced coffee, coffee with whipped cream or milk, and many other varieties.

A Japanese peculiarity is the 'cure' in which they sit immersed in coffee and pineapple. This combination is supposed to create a sauna effect and is regarded as being extremely invigorating!

GREAT BRITAIN/COFFEE

In the heyday of English coffee houses coffee was sometimes flavoured with wine, ale, butter and spices, and was the favourite beverage of all and sundry, rich and poor alike. A resurgence of this interest came in the 1950s with the arrival from Italy of the coffee bar and its frothy coffee sold in clear glass cups. Sadly, this new popularity faded away almost as quickly as it had emerged.

Notorious for drinking pale watery brews, the British are once again becoming more aware of coffee and are improving their coffee brewing techniques. More people now drink real coffee, possibly owing to the increase in foreign travel, specialist shops throughout the country and, perhaps, to the arrival of coffee bags which allow even lazy souls to brew good coffee as easily as making tea! Whatever the reason, the British are once again on the way to becoming the connoisseur coffee drinkers that they once were.

USA/COFFEE

It is to the Americans that we are eternally grateful for inventing the coffee break without which modern life would be unimaginable. Coffee in America began its life as a patriotic symbol and quickly became the nation's favourite drink. Coffee pots were an integral part of the gold rush and many a cowboy found his coffee tin as indispensable as his horse!

Coffee is drunk across this vast continent in all manners and forms but the favourite method seems to be that of the percolator which produces a hot and slightly bitter brew. Served in warm cups, drunk black, with milk or cream, sometimes with sugar or sweetener, this brew is truly an all-time winner!

per person per day are consumed. That's a lot of coffee! Being great socializers, the Finns are constantly throwing coffee parties at which huge quantities of coffee and a mouth-watering array of sweets are served.

An old-fashioned Finn recipe for the perfect brew has an intriguing method as follows:

Prepare the coffee by the Jug Method (see page 33) and after brewing add an old piece of fish skin. This will settle and clear the coffee. Before serving, discard the skin, transfer the coffee into a pot and serve with cream, milk and sugar in the usual way.

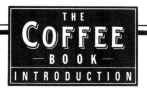

Coffee Around the World

GERMANY/KAFFEE

In the land of the *kuchen* and *torte* what could be better to accompany them than a delicious cup of coffee? The history of coffee in Germany has been quite eventful, since the time of Frederick the Great who prohibited commoners from enjoying it, to the time of the affluent bourgeois ladies who met daily for *kaffeeklatsch* (afternoon coffee) to exchange the latest gossip! Needless to say, this is a tradition which continues today although coffee afternoons are thankfully not restricted to the idle rich. The Germans' favourite accompaniment to their afternoon coffee are those exquisite pastries for which their country is justly renowned, such as Schwartzwald *torte*. Coffee in Germany is usually made by the drip method and served with condensed milk or canned cream.

Left: An open air café in Algeria not so dissimilar to those that can still be found in North Africa today.

Right: These children are enjoying *kaffeeklatsch,* the traditional German afternoon coffee break.

Opposite above left: A Franz Herden label advertising one of their specialities, 'the finest coffee blends' to be recognized by 'the sign of the golden barrel'.

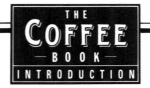
History

MANY TALES, legends and stories surround the enigma of the discovery of coffee. One favoured by historians, and perhaps the most romantic, is the tale of Kaldi, an Abyssinian goatherd. One day, sitting on a rock on the mountain slopes, Kaldi noticed that his normally docile goats had suddenly become exceptionally lively for no apparent reason. On closer inspection he discovered that they had been nibbling the bright red berries of a nearby plant. Bravely, he tasted the berries himself and after some moments found to his amazement that he felt extraordinarily uplifted and invigorated. Convinced of a miracle, he rushed to the local monastery and excitedly told his tale to the Abbot, showing him the berries that he had crammed into his leather pouch. The Abbot, instantly fearing the devil's work, flung the berries onto the fire, whereupon a wonderful and exotic aroma filled the air. Now convinced that it was God's work, the Abbot gave orders for the beans to be swiftly raked from the fire and immediately several monks rescued the beans. They were then mixed with water so that all the monks of the monastery could partake in this miracle!

Growing wild in Abyssinia and Arabia, coffee before the 10th century was eaten by the wandering tribesmen. They had discovered the alluring properties of coffee as a stimulant. The ripe fruit of the coffee plant were squashed and mixed with animal fats and shaped into round balls. These were then carried with them and eaten at intervals on their long journeys. You might say it was the original 'take-away' ('take-out'). Later on coffee was drunk, albeit in a different form from that which we know today. The berries were mixed with cold water and left to stand before drinking. The crushing of beans came at a later date and not until AD 1000, when the Arabs discovered how to boil water, did coffee become a hot drink.

The popularity of coffee spread rapidly and, not surprisingly, the Arabs were extremely proud (and jealous!) of their newly discovered beverage. They guarded their secret carefully but, with so many pilgrims in their land from near and far, it was inevitable that their sole guardianship of the mystic brew would one day be lost. Many pilgrims, having experienced the delights of coffee, smuggled fertile green beans out of their land of origin and soon coffee trees were to be found flourishing all over the surrounding areas. It was not long before the bean (and the drink) spread to more distant climes – the Arabs' monopoly had been truly broken.

Above: A botanical print of the coffee plant *(Coffea arabica).*

By the 13th century coffee had entered into the mainstream of Arabian life. It was at this time that *qahveh khaneh* (coffee houses) emerged in the towns and villages of Arabia. They quickly multiplied in number as coffee drinking became more and more popular. These *qahveh khaneh* were full of life. There was music, gambling, and a very relaxed informal atmosphere. Philosophers, politicians and tradesmen alike gathered there to discuss events of the day and exchange ideas. It was this popularity that caused rulers of the time great consternation. It seems they feared plots and intrigue against their rule and, as a result, they petitioned three times to prohibit and close down the coffee houses. All to no avail; coffee and the atmosphere of the houses in which it was served were too popular to be easily restricted. With this ever increasing popularity, coffee drinking spread into people's homes where eventually it evolved into an elaborate ceremony.

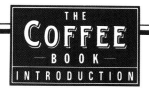

History

As coffee drinking grew in Arabia and Turkey many voyagers and traders tasted the brew and, naturally, they carried news of it back to their home shores. Consequently, word reached Europe about the delicious new drink. The first consignment of coffee arrived in Venice in 1615 from Turkey. The drink soon reached Rome where, once again, it was condemned by the clergy as the drink of the devil. Feelings about it ran so high that Pope Clement VIII asked for a sample of the brew hoping to resolve the matter once and for all. One sip revealed how delightful coffee was and he realized how foolish it would be to banish it from the Christian world forever. So he immediately blessed it. With Papal approval, the growth of coffee drinking in Italy was assured and it was not long before the first European coffee houses were opened.

The first recorded reference to coffee in England was in 1637 when a coffee house was opened in Oxford by an entrepreneur called Jacob, a Jew from Turkey. Soon afterwards, the first coffee house was opened in St Michael's Alley, Cornhill, London by Pasqua Rosee, believed to have been a Greek or an Armenian immigrant. Gradually coffee houses were to be found in many towns and cities in Great Britain. These houses were easily identifiable if not from the delectable aroma of freshly roasting coffee, than from the painted signs that hung outside them – for example, a Turkish Coffee Pot or a Sultan's Head, which were in fact the most usual. The coffee houses near the universities were frequented by locals and students alike. These quickly acquired the nickname of 'penny universities' because it was claimed that for the price of a cup of coffee – one penny – a student gained more knowledge than he ever could from reading books. How much validity there was to this claim we shall never know but the popularity of coffee houses among the student population is

Above: The coffee crop being harvested in Brazil in 1823.

beyond dispute and little has changed in this respect for 400 years.

Until the late 17th century almost all coffee came from Arabia. The Arabs attempted to maintain their fierce control over coffee supplies, forbidding seeds to be removed from the country unless they were roasted. This measure theoretically ensured that no seeds with germinating qualities would escape. Naturally, it was absolutely forbidden for foreigners to visit the plantations. However, as one would expect of such a special and popular drink, this control soon became impossible to maintain. After countless abortive attempts Dutch spies finally succeeded in stealing plants from Arabia and began to cultivate them in Java with great success. The fiercely guarded monopoly of the Arabs was finally broken. From then on, coffee was grown in Dutch hot houses and from there it was freely distributed throughout Europe.

In 1723 a dashing young captain in the French navy called de Clieu, while on leave in Paris, decided on a whim to take a coffee plant back with him to Martinique where he was stationed. Having successfully stolen a particularly hardy-looking seedling he carefully smuggled it aboard his southerly bound ship, little knowing what hazards lay in store on this eventful journey. Only two days from port a Dutch agent, unbeknown to our hero, tried to sabotage the plant by feeding it with contaminated water but Captain de Clieu caught the sinister Dutchman in the act. Later, the ship was besieged by pirates and, if this was not enough to deter anyone, the ship was hit by a fierce tempest only half a day from its final destination. All these potential disasters overcome, de Clieu planted his treasured seedling in the warm fertile soil of Martinique and the brave but cautious captain placed three of his men on permanent guard around the solitary plant! All turned out well, however, and de Clieu's efforts were amply

History

Above: The Café des Patriotes was a French coffee house which was popular during the French Revolution.

rewarded. His hardy seedling went on to flourish and multiply with extraordinary rapidity so that by 1777 there were 18 million coffee trees on the island.

It was the occasion of a boundary dispute between the rival coffee producing countries of Dutch and French Guiana which enabled Brazil to acquire a few of the highly prized coffee seedlings. On being asked to settle the dispute, Brazil sent a young officer named Palheta who, thanks to his native cunning and charming way with ladies, not only resolved the dispute but also managed by seducing the Governor's wife to acquire from her some of the much desired coffee seedlings. At a banquet given in his honor, the Governor's wife presented him with a bouquet of flowers in front of the assembled company. A charming gesture indeed, because hidden in the colourful bouquet were the green coffee seedlings which Brazil so coveted! Thus began one of the greatest coffee producing empires.

Coffee arrived in North America by courtesy of the Dutch and, in particular, New Amsterdam in 1660. Four years later the British took possession of New Amsterdam and renamed it New York. By this time coffee drinking had caught on among the inhabitants and had soon replaced beer at breakfast time to the eternal benefit of the collective health of the American nation!

The first coffee houses in New York were modelled on their London counterparts. In reality they were more like taverns; they had rooms for rent, served meals and sold ale, wine, hot chocolate and tea, as well as coffee! The more important houses had meeting rooms where all types of public and private business were conducted, such as auctions. Gradually it became common for men to carry on their business at the coffee house and adjourn to the tavern for entertainment once business was completed.

At first in New York, coffee was only available for the more affluent members of society. Tea, on the other hand, was far more popular and at one time appeared to be gaining favour among all levels of society to the detriment of coffee. This all changed however, when, in 1773, King George of England imposed a tax on tea and the American colonists spontaneously broke into revolt. Still incensed by the Stamp Act crisis of 1763, the citizens of Boston, dressed as Indians, boarded the English merchant vessels lying in the harbour and emptied their entire cargoes of tea into the ocean. Known as the Boston Tea Party, this famous historical event forged the Americans' strong bond with coffee. It soon became the national beverage – a position it still holds today!

Growing

HAT IS THIS BEAN that isn't a bean but is actually the pip of a cherry-like fruit? Cherry-like, but it is not in any way related to the cherry! It is, of course, the fruit of the coffee plant, which grows and flourishes in the tropical belt girdling the earth, between 25° north and 30° south.

The coffee plant is something of a botanical oddity mainly because the best coffee is cultivated in areas where it does not grow wild. They also thrive in a rather odd soil type consisting of composed and de-composed mould (mold), organic matter and disintegrated volcanic rock. In Hawaii, coffee grows in soil that is totally composed of volcanic rock, where-as in Brazil it is the famous red soil that nourishes the plants.

The coffee tree or shrub is capable of growing up to 30 ft in height but it is usually pruned and maintained at a height of 4 to 6 ft, which is best suited for harvesting and is also conducive to good flavoured beans. The plant bears deep green, glossy leaves which grow in alternating pairs on the stalks. Another unusual characteristic of the coffee plant is its ability to produce ripe and unripe fruit and flowers simultaneously, at various times throughout the year. The scent of its delicate white blossoms is often likened to orange blossom or jasmine.

Trees that grow from seedlings take four to six years before producing fruit. However, once mature, the trees produce blossom which soon withers and within two months clusters of berries appear in their place. These small berries gradually ripen into a deep red.

Each berry is covered with a sweet pulp which normally contains two beans or seeds. Inside this pulp, the beans are coated with a tough husk called parchment and underneath that is the inner protection or silver skin as it is called. If there is only one bean or seed in the cherry then this is known as a Peaberry and has a characteristically rounded shape. While the average plantation tree has a life expectancy of approximately 40 years, some have been

Below: A plantation of young coffee trees in Colombia.
Inset: Coffee seeds growing in a coffee nursery in Brazil.

Growing

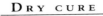

known to live for 100 years still bearing fruit! A tree is considered to be in the prime of life when it is between 10 to 15 years old. A good coffee tree in a productive year can yield 12 lb of coffee berries which is the equivalent of 4 to 5 lb of coffee beans.

Different methods of harvesting are used from country to country. Surprisingly, mechanization is not widespread at the present time and indeed the ideal coffee harvester has yet to be invented. Harvesting time on the plantations is typically extremely hectic and all able bodies are called in to pick the berries which ripen at different times on each plant. For this reason it is necessary to visit each plant several times in order to pick the berries at the correct degree of ripeness.

There are two main methods of preparing or 'curing' the bean; the Wet method and the Dry method. The former is used for quality beans, while the Dry method is utilized for less aromatic beans, being simpler and requiring less expensive machinery.

WET CURE

After initial washing, the berries are placed in machines that remove the outer fruit pulp. This process exposes the sticky inner protective coat which surrounds the parchment. The berries are then soaked in tanks of water to loosen the covering and are left to ferment for between 12 to 24 hours. Fresh water is then sprayed over the berries until the sticky protective coating is completely removed and the water runs away quite clean. The berries are then dried in the sun on mats or sometimes, more quickly, in drying machines. Finally, a machine called a huller removes the parchment and silver skin exposing the 'green bean'.

Examples of fine washed coffee are Colombian, Costa Rican and Kenyan.

DRY CURE

This method is the oldest and most natural way of curing coffee and three-fifths of all the world's coffee is still prepared in this manner. The berries are washed and then spread out in the hot sunshine in thin layers on mats for 2 to 3 weeks. During this time fermentation occurs and the beans are raked several times a day to ensure even drying. When they are completely dried the beans are tumbled into a milling machine which speeds up the removal of the dried hulk parchment and silver skin.

In the Yemen and Ethiopia the coffee berries are allowed to dry and shrivel on the coffee trees. They are then left until they fall naturally onto cloths spread out under the trees or sometimes they are given a helping shake by anxious plantation workers! Once the debris is collected and sifted to remove all the dust, leaves and twigs, the dry method of curing can then take place. Incredibly, a coffee taster, known in the trade as a cuptaster, can detect by the taste of the coffee in his cup whether this method of harvesting has taken place.

The green polished beans are now graded and packed into sacks which are stamped with the symbols of the plantation, the association and the shipper, and the coffee is now ready for shipment to various destinations in distant parts of the world.

There are two major species of commercial coffee, Arabica and Robusta:

Above: A coffee worker at the end of the day in the Ivory Coast.
Opposite: Coffee beans being sorted in Indonesia.
Opposite inset: Coffee beans being winnowed, separating the cherries from the twigs and leaves.

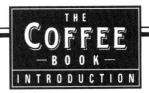

Growing

COFFEA ARABICA
(ARABICA COFFEE)

Arabica coffee is the most widely cultivated coffee and constitutes 75 per cent of all commercial coffees sold. This species of tree grows best on steep mountain slopes, requires heavy rainfall and ample shade to aid its growth.

The bean produced is harder than other types, but it has a superior flavour which is richer, tastier and more aromatic. It also has the ability to pollinate itself which makes for a better pedigree, with fewer mutations and variations over the years.

This plant requires well-drained volcanic soil, two hours of sunshine a day and, consequently, shade. In Ethiopia shade is available from larger trees whereas in Hawaii, cloud offers this natural protection.

COFFEA CANEPHORA
(ROBUSTA COFFEE)

This coffee shrub is extremely hardy and its cultivation is possible at significantly lower altitudes than Arabica coffee, some plants growing below 3,000 feet. It can survive with far less rain than other species and is also hardy enough to resist most diseases. Although Robusta beans blend well with Arabica, its own flavour is not comparable to that of Arabica. Having less flavour, Robusta is naturally cheaper than Arabica. This means that the cheaper coffee that you buy has more than 50 per cent Robusta beans in the blend and the cheapest of all coffees will be completely Robusta. Robusta coffee is grown in West and Central Africa, East Africa and Asia.

Top left: Removing the pulp from the cherry during the wet processing method.
Above left: Coffee cherries being dried using the dry processing method in a village in the Ivory Coast.

Opposite above: Arabica coffee beans from El Salvador (*left*) and Robusta from Angola (*right*).
Opposite right: A Kenyan coffee liquoring department whose responsibility is quality control and the testing of blends.

Growing

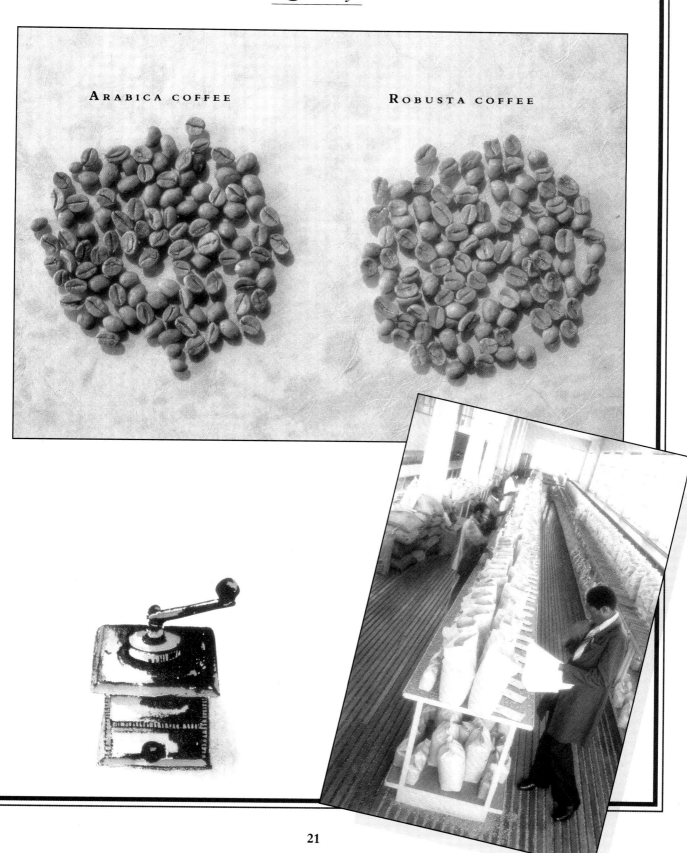

ARABICA COFFEE   ROBUSTA COFFEE

Country

SPOILT BY SUCH a multiplicity of choice, you should ultimately rely on your own taste when selecting coffee for drinking at home. Although there are no hard and fast rules when it comes to choosing your coffee, the following guidelines may help you.

Firstly be adventurous! There are so many different blends that you are bound to come across a delicious one which you would never have discovered if you stick to one particular blend. Why not keep a stock of your favourite blends and, at the same time, experiment with others? Secondly, try to find a knowledgeable supplier who you can rely on to stock the best quality range of coffee. Coffee is susceptible to the rigours of climate as well as being affected by different types of soil, cultivation, picking, processing, storage and transportation with the result that even beans from the same country may differ widely in quality. Choosing a good supplier should help to eliminate the risk of indifferent and variable standards.

Just as connoisseurs of wine have their own vocabulary to determine the contents of their glass, so too have coffee tasters. Here are a few of the more common terms used:

ACIDY This does not necessarily indicate the actual degree of acidity in the bean but refers to the sharp and pleasing taste that is neither sour nor sweet.

BODY This refers to the taste sensation as the flavour settles on the tongue. It is synonymous with richness of flavour and aroma. A thin, watery tasting coffee with little flavour is said to lack body.

HARSH Quite self explanatory! An unpleasant taste once described as 'akin to raw weeds'. This is characteristic of Robusta coffees. A few coffee drinkers prefer a hint of this harshness in their blend.

WINY A taste that, according to some, is reminiscent of well-hung pheasant. This taste is obtained from beans that have been fermented.

This short introduction to coffee tasters' terminology should assist you in communicating your choice! The list of countries that follows is of those that produce coffee, and includes descriptions and typical characteristics of the different varieties.

Around the World

ANGOLA Mostly Robusta coffee. Strong flavour but little character.

BRAZIL Best bean is Bourbon Santos; smooth and sweet with medium body producing a solidly acceptable brew.

CAMEROON 70 per cent Robusta, 30 per cent Arabica. Arabica beans are mellow, sweet-drinking coffees. The rounded Peaberries and giant 'elephant' beans are sorted and marketed separately.

COLOMBIA All coffee produced is Arabica. The finest is Medellin; less acidity than most Colombian coffees and rich in flavour.

COSTA RICA All coffee is Arabica. Very mild with nutty background. Full bodied and rich.

DOMINICAN REPUBLIC Coffee known as Santos Domingos. Good body and pleasantly sweet.

ECUADOR Perhaps the highest Arabica plantations in the world. Called Ecuadors, coffee is sharp with woody flavour, lacking in body. Usually blended.

EL SALVADOR All coffees are Arabica. Top two grades have good acidity and body. Mild in flavour, not overly aromatic.

ETHIOPIA Hawar is best known; smooth strong flavour. Characteristics include a winy pungence and an exquisite aroma.

GUATEMALA All coffees are Arabica. Well flavoured with snap and zest. A dry aroma. Best grades are Antigua and Coban.

HAITI Mellow with mild sweetness. Full bodied and pungent.

Country

HAWAII Best known is Kona. Strong flavoured, full bodied and mellow.

INDIA Best known is Mysore. Rich and strong. Good body.

INDONESIA Home of Java. Thick mellow character. Heavy bodied. Blended with Yemeni-Java. Other fine beans are Celebes and Sumatra.

JAMAICA Renowned for Blue Mountain. Exceptionally sweet tasting, mellow and wonderfully aromatic. Very small crop produces famous coffee.

KENYA Mild coffee of Arabica variety. Smooth and round taste, fine aroma.

MEXICO Arabica coffee, wonderful aroma, tends towards sharpness. Best varieties are Coatepec, Jalapa and Pluma.

NICARAGUA Good body, biting acidity.

PERU Best is Chanchamayo; mild flavour with excellent body, slightly sweet.

PUERTO RICO Not exported. Sweet flavour and full, rich body. If you want to approximate the taste, try a good French roast or a blend of French and an Italian dark roast.

TANZANIA Producer of two-thirds of all Arabica coffee. Rich and mellow with a delicate body. Exporter of Peaberry grade.

VENEZUELA Marketed as Maracaibo. Flavourful, rich, delicate winy taste. Light bodied, mellow and slightly sweet. Softly aromatic.

YEMEN Oldest and most famous is Mocha. A rich almost chocolate-flavoured coffee. Its name has also been given to the flavour of coffee and chocolate in combination. Smooth and piquant.

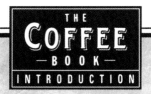
A Selection of Coffees

RAW　　　　**ROAST**　　　　**GROUND**

Jamaican Blue Mountain (Arabica) is three times the price of other coffees – the crop is very small. Served medium roast and filter fine ground for a filter, it is smooth and mild, ideal for drinking black even if this is not your normal preference.

  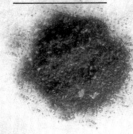

This Nicaraguan (Arabica) coffee has been medium roasted and normally ground for preparation by the jug method. This coffee is a common constituent of Mountain blends and has good body and biting acidity.

The Colombian Medellin Excelso (Arabica) is medium to dark roast and has been coarsely ground for percolators. It is sold pure or in various Columbian blends.

Brazilian Santos (Arabica) is medium roasted and normally ground for preparation by the jug method. It is sold pure and in blends and is smooth and sweet of medium body.

The dark roasted Brazilian Santos (Robusta) has been finely ground and is filter fine. It is used only in blends.

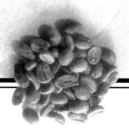  

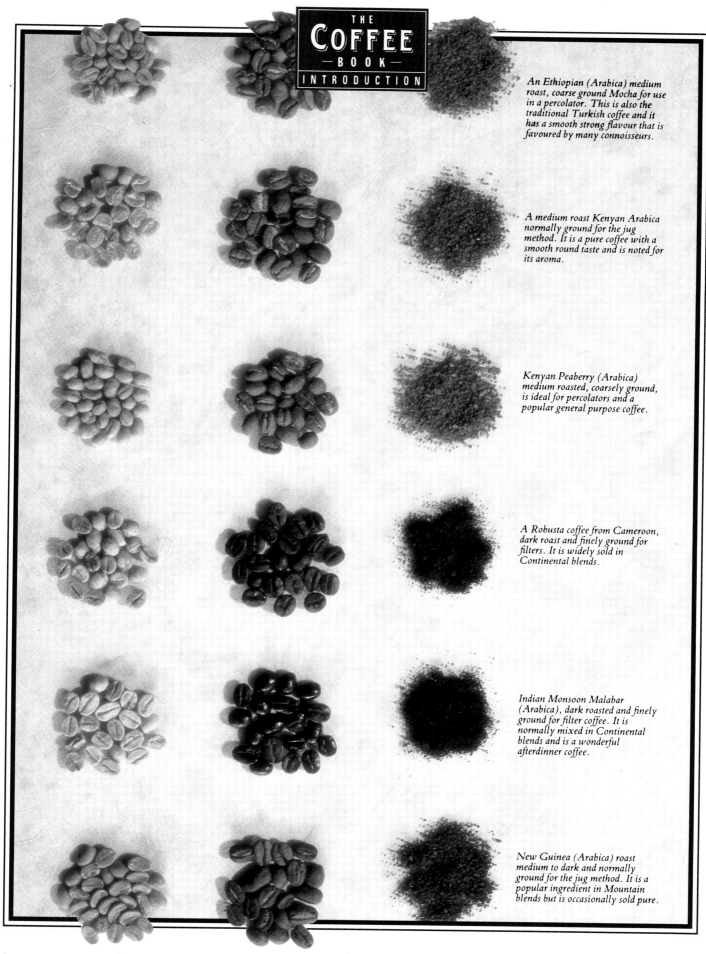

An Ethiopian (Arabica) medium roast, coarse ground Mocha for use in a percolator. This is also the traditional Turkish coffee and it has a smooth strong flavour that is favoured by many connoisseurs.

A medium roast Kenyan Arabica normally ground for the jug method. It is a pure coffee with a smooth round taste and is noted for its aroma.

Kenyan Peaberry (Arabica) medium roasted, coarsely ground, is ideal for percolators and a popular general purpose coffee.

A Robusta coffee from Cameroon, dark roast and finely ground for filters. It is widely sold in Continental blends.

Indian Monsoon Malabar (Arabica), dark roasted and finely ground for filter coffee. It is normally mixed in Continental blends and is a wonderful afterdinner coffee.

New Guinea (Arabica) roast medium to dark and normally ground for the jug method. It is a popular ingredient in Mountain blends but is occasionally sold pure.

25

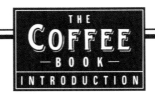
Which Coffee?

PURE COFFEES

KNOWN as 'aristocrats', Arabica beans are indeed the connoisseurs' favourite. The coffee trade usually refer to these coffees as pure or original. These classifications usually mean that the coffee beans have come from one particular plantation or one particular area within one country (see list below). However, the terms can also indicate a combination of Arabica beans from different areas of the same country. country.

The following list of the most well known pure coffees will clarify some of the distinguishing features.

BRAZILIAN SANTOS A high quality bean grown in São Paulo region. It is smooth, full bodied with only a slight bitterness or acidity. Derives its flavour from the iron rich soil – *terra roxa* – in which it is grown.

COLOMBIAN MEDELLIN EXCELSO Has less acidity than most Colombian coffees. Full of aroma, a light flavourful coffee.

COSTA RICAN A very mild coffee, full bodied with a nutty background. Very smooth and satisfying.

ETHIOPIAN MOCHA This coffee comes from the name of the original coffee plant. It is a smooth, well-matured coffee with a distinctive aroma. Its flavour is reminiscent of high pheasant, hence the trade term 'gamey'. Excellent after dinner coffee.

JAMAICAN BLUE MOUNTAIN The world's most expensive coffee. Ninety-eight per cent of its harvest is exported to Japan. The remaining 2 per cent is used in blends and, in fact, there are many so-called Blue Mountain blends available. Beware of imitations! Genuine Blue Mountain beans are certified as such by the Jamaican Coffee Industry Board.

JAVA Well matured before roasting. Unique slightly smoky flavour. Useful after dinner blend.

KENYAN Rates among the world's finest coffee. Strong flavour, sharp acidity and fine aroma. Suitable for people who like coffee with a bite.

MYSORE A southern Indian coffee. Very rich in flavour, often described as 'winy'. Full bodied, sometimes blended with Mocha, resulting in a blend known as Mysore Mocha.

NICARAGUA An ideal breakfast coffee, mild and often used in blends.

TANZANIAN KILIMANJARO A coffee with a distinctive, well-balanced flavour. Stronger than those coffees grown in Central America.

SUMATRA This coffee is often dark-roasted and has a heavy mellow flavour with little acidity.

BLENDING

BLENDING is usually a marriage between Arabica and Robusta coffees. The majority of coffees available for the mass market tend to be a blend of a number of different varieties. The main aim of blending is to produce a desired taste, flavour and aroma which can be regularly repeated. Without doubt, blending is an art, whether for the mass market or for the specialist trade. Naturally, the results achieved by this art are a very closely guarded secret. Each type of bean has its own special strengths and weaknesses, and when they are blended they either combine or neutralize a number of different coffee characteristics. Herein lies the art of blending. A good acidity coffee may lack body, or one with body may not have a desirable taste. When the beans are blended, the characteristics which are required, such as aroma, acidity, body and colour, can be emphasized.

Faced with such a spectrum of choice at your local specialist shop, a good start is to ask for their house blend. This may contain a balanced number of mild and strong coffees. These mixtures are usually combinations of beans from Africa, Brazil, Colombia, Mexico, Central America and Indonesia. Some blends contain four kinds of coffee, whereas others may contain twelve. There is certainly no standard house or speciality blend. When you are tempted to try a new blend, it is sensible to buy the smallest amount possible in order to find out whether or not it is to your taste.

Which Coffee?

Above: A selection of popular coffees. From top left clockwise: Italian No. 1, Colombian Medellin No. 1, decaffeinated, Brazilian mild, Javan and Kenyan.

The store's house blend will often be designed to appeal to all and sundry, it is unlikely to be particularly individual and you may quickly wish to progress on to something more exotic. As a starting point to a more specialist taste, you could always ask for an additional blend to be added, e.g. a dark or aromatic roast. You are now on the road to becoming a coffee connoisseur!

Once the frontier of drinking real coffee has been broken there should be nothing to hold you back. Be adventurous; sample and experiment with the blends available to you. It would be a pity not to pursue your new interest simply because one particular blend is not to your taste.

Having gained more confidence in your ability to select coffee, you may wish to start blending your own coffee. This is not such a daunting task as it sounds. After trial and error you will be able to distinguish body, acidity and flavour in coffee. You should also know which qualities you prefer in coffee and what your blending aims are. By this stage you will know whether you want an all-round coffee or a heavy mellow coffee, or even a light coffee with body as well.

If, by now, you have a favourite coffee which lacks that certain something, combine it with a coffee that has in extreme form what your favourite lacks. Here are some additions that might help you.

☛ Richness and body: add Sumatran or Javan.
☛ Sweetness: add Venezuelan or Haitian.
☛ Extra sweetness (or to dull a bright coffee): add an aged coffee, for example, a mature Javan or Mysore.
☛ Flavour and aroma: add Sumatran, Celebes or Colombian.
☛ Brightness and acidity: add Costa Rican or any of the good Central American coffees.

You can be as imaginative as you like but remember there is one important rule; do not combine two coffees that are distinctive or extreme in the same way.

The blends that follow are available in most specialist stores although remember that they are only a small selection of many.

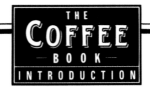

Which Coffee?

BREAKFAST A good general purpose blend combining the strength of African coffees with the mildness and body of Central American. A coffee for those who cannot decide between a mild or strong coffee!

NEAPOLITAN/ROMA These will be mixtures of Brazilian Santos and African, and finished in a heavy dark Italian roast.

MOCHA JAVA Almost every specialist store will sell what they describe as a Mocha and Java blend. Unfortunately there is probably insufficient true Javan Arabica and Mocha produced in an average year to make one cup of Mocha Java brew each for every coffee drinker in a major city. Present day Mocha is very likely to be a Mocha-style bean from Africa and the Java may, in fact, be a Java-style bean from Malay Archipelago. This is nonetheless an excellent blend of coffee.

FINE HOUSE BLEND A typical fine house blend may, for example, be based on Costa Rican, laced with a high-grown coffee such as Venezuelan with perhaps a dash of Jamaican Blue Mountain.

Your specialist store will have their own selection of pure coffees and blends from which you can decide on your own favourite. The choice is yours!

ROASTING

IT IS MIRACULOUS how virtually odourless green beans spring to life when roasted! This process reduces the moisture in the green beans which, in turn, releases the aromatic oils resulting in the characteristic flavours and aromas that we associate with coffee.

A century ago there were no large scale commercial roasters and all coffee was roasted either in the home or by a local storekeeper who had his own batch roaster. This machine consisted of a perforated metal drum in which the beans were rotated over heated charcoal. Nowadays, charcoal is usually substituted by gas or electricity although a few stores today still possess this old fashioned type of roaster – proof that the old fashioned techniques cannot be bettered.

Home roasting was usually performed over an open fire in anything that came to hand from frying pans to pudding bowls. Some devices were known as coffee burners – presumably the name did not denote the condition and taste of the beans! When Frederick the Great of Germany banned coffee consumption from most of the populace, his 'coffee sniffers' were able to detect the law breakers by the aroma of home roasting beans. Not a difficult or an unpleasant task by any means.

In the last 50 years the ever increasing spread of coffee drinking has given rise to a large scale industry in commercial roasting (and blending). The commercial roasters naturally utilize vast machines combined with extremely sophisticated roasting techniques. In large scale commercial roasting, the beans are exposed to very high temperatures for very short periods – approximately five minutes at 204 to 260°C/400 to 500°F. Immediately after this process, the beans are cooled mechanically with air jets (or sometimes sprayed water) preventing the beans from over-cooking.

Latest developments in the roasting process include total control of production by computer. In some new computerized processes the actual roasting time is only one minute. While this results in greater efficiency, it is doubtful whether these techniques produce a better flavour than traditional methods.

Specialist shops often have their roasting equipment situated in a prominent position, for example, in the shop window. This is not only to allow passers-by to watch the process but also because air vents are usually situated so as to allow the intoxicating aroma of freshly roasted coffee to waft out into the street. The innocent pedestrian is enticed over the threshold of the shop, lured as if by a siren to purchase ¼ lb/100 g of Mocha Java, or whatever.

The roaster in the specialist coffee shop carries an immense responsibility. His skill can either make or ruin the roast, for a delay of only a few seconds can mean the difference between a medium and a dark roast. Great experience is required at this stage in the bean's life and some roasters seem to have a sixth sense which tells them exactly when the roasting beans are ready to be cooled.

There are a number of stages in roasting and, although terms and degrees of roasting are interpreted differently, the following types are generally recognized:

LIGHT OR PALE ROAST/
CINNAMON ROAST

Suitable for milder beans, these roasts allow them to release their full delicate flavour and aroma. The finished surface is light brown and dry. They are recommended for breakfast coffees because they complement milk. Surprisingly, these roasts do not contain cinnamon.

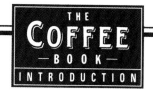

Which Coffee?

MEDIUM ROAST/AMERICAN ROAST

This is usually a general purpose roast which produces a slightly stronger, rather sweet and rich flavour. The bean is roasted to a medium brown colour resulting in a dry, rather than oily, surface.

FULL ROAST/HIGH ROAST

These beans are roasted lightly for a slightly longer period than medium roast. The bean is dark brown and shows no oil on the surface. This coffee produces a deep, hearty brew.

DOUBLE OR HIGH ROAST/
CONTINENTAL ROAST

This is a dark brown roast with an oily surface that has more tang than a full roast and a strong, bitter kick. It should preferably be drunk black.

ITALIAN ROAST/ESPRESSO ROAST

This is the highest, heaviest, darkest roast cooked to a point just short of burning which leaves the surface of the bean shiny, oily and black in colour. It is preferred for the extra fine grind that is required for *espresso* coffee making equipment.

DRY ROAST

Not an actual roast but a method whereby the freshly roasted beans are allowed to cool naturally in the surrounding air, as opposed to cooling by water. The advantage of air drying is that it does not affect the flavour significantly. The same cannot be said of water drying which tends to be used in large scale commercial roasting. Obviously the best coffee is dry roasted.

HOME ROASTING

The main aim of home roasting, apart from the sheer enjoyment of doing it yourself, is to achieve beans that are evenly roasted without scorching. When buying green beans from your local specialist, remember that they swell when roasted so do not be surprised if your package looks small.

When home roasting, use an old heavy pan and cover the base with one layer of green beans. Take care not to attempt too many beans at one time as this results in uneven roasting.

The Café du Commerce is one of the most popular café names in France, perhaps because they were and are frequented still by commercial travellers. Some cafés traded originally as barbers and wig-fitters and first served coffee to relieve their clients' boredom.

Cover the frying pan so as to contain the aroma, and heat on a medium to high flame so the beans develop without burning. Shake the pan constantly and turn the beans over so that they are exposed to the heat on all sides. Once they start to brown, they will develop quite rapidly. When a good brown colour is achieved crack one bean open; it should break easily and the fragments should be brown throughout. If the bean is thoroughly roasted inside as well as outside you have been successful. Remember, it is not a particularly easy process and don't be too ambitious at first, so try to aim for a medium brown colour.

Remove the beans from the pan and cool quickly, either by placing the pan on a marble slab or dipping it into a shallow water bath. The surrounding water will help cool the beans quickly and stop the roasting process.

If you are bitten by the home roasting bug and wish to use a more sophisticated method, you will find that there are a variety of home roasting devices available on the market. These roasters consist of a one-piece covered frying pan with an opening, a built-in stirring mechanism and a handle that is designed not to overheat. One major tip is to ensure adequate ventilation in the kitchen where you are carrying out your home roasting. Failure to do so could leave the room smelling unpleasant for days afterwards, even though, of course, the heavy

Which Coffee?

aromatic smoke is pleasant at first. The beans are now ready for storing in airtight containers.

Coffee beans will keep fresh nearly three times as long as ground coffee. Whereas ground coffee loses its freshness, taste and aroma in just ten days, beans will keep for another two weeks. Whether you buy whole beans or ground coffee, you must store it in an airtight container – a glass jar with a rubber seal is ideal – in a cool, dark place.

Although there is no advantage in storing coffee in a refrigerator, coffee beans can be kept in a freezer for several months. Wrap them well and make sure they are sealed away from other flavours. There is no need to thaw beans before grinding and brewing. Ground coffee can also be stored in a freezer for up to one month and, like the beans, requires no thawing before brewing.

GRINDING

T IS A FACT that for many true connoisseurs the ritual of grinding fresh coffee beans is sublime. The golden rule is never to grind more than you are going to brew at any one time.

Apart from the actual brewing, grinding is crucial for the proper release of precious aromatic oils and aromas that make freshly ground coffee what it is. From the moment of grinding these flavours and aromas start to deteriorate and, therefore, it is important to brew your coffee within seconds of grinding. Different methods of brewing coffee require different grinds. The fineness of the grind is crucial because it is related to the amount of time the water will be in contact with the coffee during the selected methods of brewing.

As a guide, the following grinds can be used with various types of coffee making machines.

PULVERIZED This grind is only used for making proper Turkish coffee in an *ibrik*.

VERY FINE Used for filter coffee makers. Coffee for filters should not be pulverized as this allows lengthy extraction and hence a bitter taste.

FINE ESPRESSO This grind is for the *espresso* machines in which hot steam is forced through the coffee grounds. Again, too fine a grind could not only result in a bitter taste, but also cause a blockage and subsequent damage to the coffee machine.

MEDIUM Coffee ground to this degree is very adaptable because it can be used in percolators, vacuum coffee makers and for the jug method.

Above: Three popular types of grinder (*from left to right*) electric (*left*) and manual (*centre and right*).

COARSE Coarse ground coffee is only truly suitable for percolators which have aluminium (aluminum) filters, used to strain the infused liquid. Too fine a grind results in 'muddy' coffee.

Coffee grinders come in all shapes and sizes. The most basic and primitive kind is the mortar and pestle which was used by the Arabs to grind their coffee, hundreds of years ago before coffee was even heard of in the western world. Grinding by this method is an extremely slow process and you will not be able to achieve just the grind you want unless you are very skilful or exceptionally lucky!

Thankfully, the Turks developed very early on an automatic grinding apparatus made out of steel and with a crank. Today's basic coffee grinder differs little from the machines which first appeared during the 15th century. The coffee beans are fed either by a funnel or by a slotted screw between two corrugated metal discs, one stationary and the other turned by the same crank that turns the feeding screw.

The most basic types of coffee grinder are mounted on a box with a small drawer that catches the freshly ground coffee. More sophisticated, larger models can be attached to a wall and also have

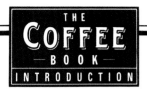
Which Coffee?

adjusting screws that regulate how close the plates come to each other, giving different degrees of grind. Electric grinders require the least effort! Small electric blades grind coffee to any degree at the touch of a button. The blades whirl around at a fantastic speed, chopping up the beans while creating air currents that keep the grinds coming back to the blades. Release the button and check to see if the grind is precisely what you want and stop. If not keep going until it is satisfactory. Although extremely convenient, modern electric grinders are prone to breakdown and will not have a particularly long life, whereas the traditional grinder should last a lifetime and longer. Some people think that there is something inherently more satisfying about grinding coffee beans manually.

INSTANT COFFEE

EA AND COFFEE have always been inextricably linked and no more so than in the development of instant coffee. Since the 1860s coffee processors had been trying to create a powdered coffee for the mass market but with no success. All they had managed to produce were either thick liquids or solid cakes. A Japanese chemist called Dr Sartori Kato invented a powdered tea and travelled to the United States of America to promote it. In 1899 the Americans showed little or no interest in Kato's powdered tea formula.

Although the people of Chicago were no more taken by powdered tea than others, a group of canny chemists and coffee roasters realized the potential of the idea in relation to coffee. They urged Dr Kato to try his process on coffee beans. Eureka – instant coffee was born! It was first unveiled to the general public at a Pan-American exposition held in Buffalo, New York in 1901.

While all this interest in instant coffee was being shown in the North of America, a shrewd Englishman, Mr G. Washington, who lived in Guatemala City, was being not inattentive to the world around him. Every afternoon, while sitting in the shade of his cool orange grove, he was served coffee by one of his house servants. One day he idly noticed that a soft brown powder had accumulated under the spout of his coffee pot. Moistening his fingertip, Mr Washington gently touched the powder and tasted it. It struck him, after a few moments' reflection, that this was a naturally produced instant coffee powder. Developed in the mile-high mountain climate of Guatemala, this natural marvel was soon refined and marketed as 'Red E Coffee' by the G. Washington Coffee Refining Company. You will gather that Mr Washington was more than just an observant man of leisure – he was also a clever businessman. His brand of instant coffee dominated the market from 1910 until just before World War II.

Instant coffee is generally made by two methods; freeze drying or spray drying. Both processes begin with percolation. The coffee extract that leaves the commercial percolator resembles your homemade coffee in name and colour only. To give you an idea of the difference, you probably brew 50 cups of coffee from a pound of roasted coffee beans. By contrast, the commercial coffee percolator can extract the equivalent of 100 cups per pound of roasted coffee beans! However, commercial percolation has a serious drawback; the intense pressure alters the molecular structure of the humble bean which adversely affects the aroma and flavour. Beans chosen for the instant coffee process are usually low price varieties and are mainly Robusta.

During the drying stage of instant coffee making, the more volatile of the natural flavours and aromas of coffee are driven off although similar flavours and aromas produced during percolation hydrolysis and extraction remain.

To produce instant coffee powder, the percolated liquid is dispersed into small droplets through an atomizing spray and allowed to fall in a stream of heated air. This causes the water to evaporate, leaving a powder of coffee extract. An alternative method known as freeze drying was invented in the 1960s. This method produces a superior coffee because it loses less of its natural qualities than when subjected to spray drying. Freeze drying basically consists of freezing the commercial percolated brew and removing the moisture with a vacuum pump. Recent technology has allowed significant progress in re-introducing aroma and flavour into instant coffees. Some of these new techniques include adding natural coffee oils to instant powders or granules and pumping coffee aroma gas through the powder.

Ingenious as these processes may be, the commercial instant coffee makers will never be able to produce an instant coffee that justifies the label real coffee. Admittedly, the latest freeze-drying and other techniques have produced a flavour which is incomparably superior to the products of twenty years ago, but, to the coffee connoisseur, these are only to be sipped when refusal would offend.

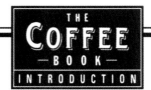
Which Coffee?

DECAFFEINATED COFFEE

OVER 150 YEARS AGO caffeine was isolated and identified as the active ingredient in coffee – the reason for its famous stimulating effect. Quantities of caffeine are also present in tea, soft drinks and chocolate. People have different levels of tolerance to caffeine which explains some of the differences in people's drinking habits! Some people seem to be able to drink a cup of black coffee before going to bed and still sleep as soon as their head hits the pillow. Others would not get a moment's sleep all night!

The aim of decaffeination is to remove caffeine from the green coffee bean without adversely affecting the flavour which develops when the beans are roasted. Caffeine, itself, is an alkaloid which when isolated in its pure form, appears as tiny white crystals. Unfortunately for coffee connoisseurs who react badly to caffeine, decaffeinated coffees tend to be inferior in taste, aroma and appearance as a result of the heating, soaking, steaming and the other processes to which the beans have been subjected.

Better quality beans contain less caffeine whereas Robusta which is used mainly for instant coffee contains the most. The decaffeination process removes approximately 97 per cent of the caffeine in coffee.

But for people who cannot drink coffee without spending the whole night wide awake, the slight loss in taste is better than being deprived of the delicious brew altogether!

Above: Typical French café fare. Coffee in France is typically drunk very black and sweet. Champagne Cognac and Liqueur de Fraise des Bois are generally reserved for more special occasions.

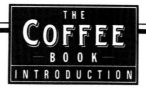

Brewing

IT IS IMPOSSIBLE to state emphatically that the perfect cup of coffee is made by any particular method of brewing. Of course, to some extent it is a matter of taste. As everybody knows, whichever method of brewing is used, coffee can taste either excellent or awful. It all depends on how carefully it has been stored, ground and brewed. The same coffee beans will produce a different flavour according to the brewing method used. Not only does individual taste vary from person to person but you may find that your favourite breakfast coffee is not your favourite after dinner coffee. In other words, the definition of the perfect cup can depend on the time of day. The following descriptions of brewing methods will enable you to make the best cup possible with whichever method you choose.

Before you dash ahead, here are a few do's and don'ts.

Do's

☛ Do keep your coffee brewing equipment clean and wash thoroughly after each use as grounds and oils soon become rancid
☛ Do use sufficient coffee (as a rough guideline, 2 tbsp per cup)
☛ Do warm the pot before brewing (this does not apply to methods of brewing where the pot itself is heated in the process)
☛ Do use fresh clean water
☛ Do use the correct grind suitable for your method of brewing
☛ Do drink the hot coffee as soon as it is made

Don'ts

☛ Do not re-use coffee grounds
☛ Do not make coffee with boiling water because the best brewing temperature of water is 2° below boiling point
☛ Do not boil coffee!

Jug Method

This method of brewing coffee is also known as steeping or open pot brewing. It is the oldest and simplest method of preparing coffee and was introduced in France in 1711. Heat a jug or pot, preferably with a lid, thoroughly with hot water. Pour this water away and spoon in the required amount of coarse ground coffee. Add hot water and stir thoroughly. Leave to infuse for three to five minutes. Pour the coffee through a strainer, being careful not to disturb the grounds which have settled at the bottom of the pot.

Cafetière or Plunger

The *cafetière* or plunger method of coffee brewing is really a modification of the jug method. The pot consists of a heatproof glass jar in a stand and with a plunger/filter mechanism attached to the lid. The pot is pre-warmed, the measured amount of medium ground coffee is added and topped with hot water. Let the coffee infuse for four minutes and then depress the plunger very carefully. Serve immediately.

There are some drawbacks to this method. After brewing for four minutes the coffee will not be particularly hot and the plunger cannot completely separate the brew from the grounds. However, it does look very attractive and with this method you can brew your coffee at the table.

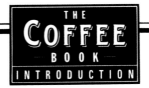

Brewing

VACUUM OR GLASS BALLOON

Although no longer fashionable, this method of coffee brewing is sometimes used by caterers. It is rather time consuming and very susceptible to breakage because both bowls are made of glass. Spoon into the top bowl the required amount of medium to fine ground coffee. The bottom bowl is filled with fresh cold water. Insert the top bowl into the rim of the bottom bowl and twist together to create a seal. This seal creates a vacuum. Put the machine onto heat and bring to the boil. The water will then rise through the funnel and pass into the top bowl. Stir and infuse for one to four minutes. When the pot is removed from the heat, a vacuum forms in the lower bowl with the result that the brewed coffee filters back down. Remove the upper bowl and serve.

INSTANT COFFEE

It is just possible to improve the taste of instant coffee if it is made in a pot. Heat the pot first with boiling water and spoon in the coffee – one heaped teaspoon/ 5 g per cup. Add hot water, stir and serve in pre-heated cups.

THE NEAPOLITAN FLIP

As you will see this little pot is aptly named. This method of making coffee is very popular in Italy where it is called the *Napoletana machinetta*. The machine is two-tiered with a coffee basket in the middle. The coffee basket is filled with finely ground dark roast coffee. The bottom container is filled with water and the serving container, complete with spout, is screwed on top, upside down. The machine is then placed on the heat and, when the water boils, steam escapes from a valve just below the coffee basket. At this point the pot is removed from the heat and flipped over to allow the hot water to run through the coffee into the serving container which is now the bottom pot.

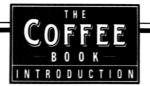

Brewing

THE FILTER

This classic way of making coffee is the most satis-factory of all the drip methods. It is not expensive to buy the basic components; a pot, a filter and paper or cloth filter liners. The resulting coffee is sparkling. Preheat the coffee pot which can be made of heat-resistant glass, porcelain or enamel.

Place the cone-shaped paper or cloth liner into the filter and place on top of your chosen pot. Spoon in the required amount of finely ground coffee and slowly pour on the hot water. At first, pour just enough to moisten the coffee. This allows the grounds to expand and water passes through more slowly resulting in maximum extraction. Pour through the remaining water. When the water has filtered through, remove the filter, replace the coffee pot lid and serve.

The most successful of the automatic coffeemakers work on this principle and machines are available for use both commercially and in the home.

THE AUTOMATIC FILTER MACHINE

These machines are very popular and home models can make between two and twelve cups of coffee at any one time. It is best to follow the instructions that apply to your machine but the basic method remains the same. Fill the water reservoir with the required amount of fresh cold water and measure out the finely ground coffee into the filter. Switch on and the machine will brew the coffee for you.

Coffee can be kept hot on these machines, but do not leave it for any longer than 45 minutes otherwise the coffee could taste like 'old tyres', according to one connoisseur!

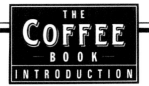

Brewing

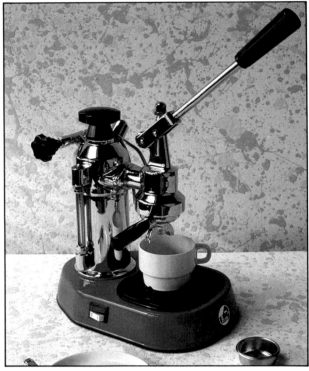

ESPRESSO/MOKA POTS

The famous Italian *espresso* machine was invented by Achille Gaggia in 1946. This wonderful machine produces that exquisite coffee known as *espresso* and also *cappuccino*. The principle behind *espresso* is pressure. Because of the pressure created in the machine, the water boils at a higher temperature than normal and steam is then forced through the grounds producing a stronger extraction of coffee than that of boiling water. Domestic Gaggias and their equivalents are available today but they are expensive. However, you can make *espresso* coffee at home with a *moka* type pot. This works on the same steam principle as the larger, more sophisticated machines and produces *espresso* to the same standard as the Gaggia but at far less cost. The coffee is made by filling the base with fresh cold water and the coffee basket with very fine high roast coffee, packed down lightly and evenly. Screw the top and base together and place over the heat. The characteristic 'gurgle and woosh' tells you that the coffee is ready. Remove from the heat and serve. It is inadvisable to leave the pot on the heat when there is no water in it. The rubber and washer needs replacing occasionally.

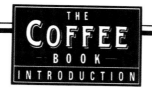
Brewing

TURKISH COFFEE

Turkish coffee is the name applied, although not quite accurately, to all Middle Eastern coffee. In Turkey it is brewed with great ritual and ceremoniously drunk in little sips while emitting a slight sucking sound. Regional variations include flavouring the coffee with spices, altering the type of beans used and the number of times it is boiled.

Whatever the variation, coffee is made in an *ibrik*. Traditionally, this is a long handled small pot which is narrower at the top than at the bottom and made out of metal, usually brass. If you cannot find an *ibrik* then a small saucepan can be used. Brewing is made easier if you only make three cups at a time. The coffee should be a medium high roast and pulverized.

Spoon the required amount of sugar into the *ibrik* and add the water, bringing to the boil over a low heat. Stir in the coffee and replace on the heat. When the liquid reaches a frothy boil remove from the heat and stir. Repeat twice. On the final boil add one teaspoon (5 ml) of cold water to speed the settling of the grounds. Shake a little froth into previously warmed demitasse cups, ensuring that everyone receives some froth as it is a token of good fortune.

THE PERCOLATOR METHOD

The percolator first made its appearance in 1825 and was extremely fashionable for a time. Today it is sometimes criticized by coffee experts because it pumps boiling water repeatedly through the coffee grounds, and supposedly ruins the taste.

The percolator's main advantage is that it uses less coffee because the water acts on it for a longer time. The old style percolators could be used either on top of the stove or on the fire but the brewer had to make a mental note not to forget it. New electric percolators have thermostats that control the brewing time and ensure a good brew.

Whichever machine you use, the principles are the same. Remove the stem and coffee basket from the pot and fill with the required amount of coarsely ground coffee – most of the baskets have cup markings. Pour the required amount of fresh cold water into the pot, replace the stem and basket, and put on the lid. Gently bring to almost boiling and then reduce the heat until the coffee begins to 'perc'. Electric percolators do this automatically. Allow the coffee to percolate for six to eight minutes. Take it off the heat, remove the basket and serve.

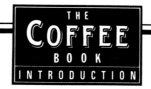

Coffee in Cooking

OFFEE IS AN INGREDIENT that adds an exotic and inspired tang to your cooking. Primarily thought of as a drink, coffee is in fact far more versatile! Most people think that it can only be used to flavour candies, desserts and drinks. However, surprising though it may seem, coffee can also be used as a marvellous and interesting complement to savoury dishes.

Coffee has tremendous adaptability and gives you the opportunity to go beyond the normal realms of savoury cooking by adding this excitingly different flavour.

Diversity is the keynote – for example, coffee adds a sublime taste to marinades, it enhances sauces and even complements curry. The recipes that follow use coffee in all its forms – freshly brewed, freshly ground coffee grains, instant coffee, coffee essence and last but not least, coffee liqueurs. All these recipes are aimed at inspiring you to further creations with coffee. Bon appétit!

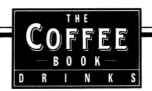

Drinks

Opposite: South Seas Café (*see page 42*).

South Seas Café

INGREDIENTS

SERVES 2

2 tbsp/30 ml Crême de Banane

2 tbsp/30 ml white rum

1 tsp/5 g brown sugar

1 cup/225 ml/8 fl oz hot black coffee

TO SERVE

6 tbsp/90 ml double (heavy) cream, lightly whipped

grated chocolate

PREPARATION

☛ Mix the Crême de Banane, white rum and sugar together. Add the hot coffee and stir well.

TO SERVE

Pour into two warmed brandy glasses. Add the cream over a spoon onto the coffee and lightly dust with grated chocolate.

Creamy Malibu Cup

INGREDIENTS

SERVES 8—10

2½ cups/550 ml/1 pt milk

4 tbsp/60 ml pineapple juice

1 cup/100 g/4 oz desiccated (shredded) coconut

2½ cups/550 ml/1 pt hot strong coffee

4 tbsp/60 ml white rum

PREPARATION

☛ Heat together the milk, pineapple juice and coconut until the liquid becomes creamy.
☛ Strain, reserve the liquid and lightly toast the coconut under the grill (broiler). Mix the hot coffee and coconut milk together and stir in the white rum.

TO SERVE

Pour into warmed cups and serve sprinkled with the toasted coconut.

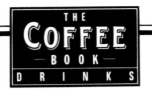
Irish Coffee

INGREDIENTS

SERVES 1

2 tbsp/30 ml Irish Whiskey

1 tsp/15 g brown sugar

⅔ cup/175 ml/¼ pt strong coffee

TO SERVE

3 tbsp/45 ml double (heavy) cream, lightly whipped

PREPARATION

☛ Warm an Irish Coffee or long glass, add the sugar and whiskey and pour on the coffee. It is important to use a strong brew so that the coffee compliments the whiskey rather than being drowned by it.

TO SERVE

Pour the cream over a spoon onto the coffee and drink the warm liquid through the cool layer of cream.

Hot Mocha

INGREDIENTS

SERVES 2

100 g/4 oz plain chocolate

2 tbsp/30 ml Kahlua

1 cup/225 ml/8 fl oz hot strong black coffee

TO SERVE

6 tbsp/90 ml double (heavy) cream, lightly whipped

chocolate beans

PREPARATION

☛ Gently melt the chocolate in a pan being careful not to burn it. Gradually add the other ingredients, except the cream and heat gently.

TO SERVE

Pour into two warmed balloon glasses. Spoon the cream onto the hot mocha and decorate with chocolate beans.

Calypso Coffee

INGREDIENTS

SERVES 6

5 cups/1 1/2 pt hot coffee

2 tbsp/30 ml white rum

4 tbsp/60 ml Tia Maria

TO SERVE

⅔ cup/150 ml/¼ pt double (heavy) cream,
lightly whipped

PREPARATION

☛ Heat all the ingredients, except the cream, but do
not boil.

TO SERVE

Warm four brandy glasses and divide the liquid
between them. Stir and add the cream, pouring it
slowly over the back of a spoon so that its weight
does not pull it straight to the bottom.

Café Brulôt Diabolique

INGREDIENTS

SERVES 6—8

8 cloves

1 piece of stick cinnamon

1 vanilla pod

thinly pared rind of 1 orange

thinly pared rind of 1 lemon

3 tbsp/45 g sugar

²/3 cup/175 ml/¼ pt brandy

5 cups/1 1/2 pt hot coffee

TO SERVE

5 tbsp/75 ml Cointreau

PREPARATION

☛ This punch can be made in a saucepan but it looks far more dramatic when made at the table. Use any deep heat resistant bowl but traditionally a silver bowl is used.

☛ Put the cloves, cinnamon, vanilla, orange and lemon rind and sugar into the bowl.

☛ Pour the brandy into a warmed ladle a little at a time and heat gently. Ignite and pour over the ingredients in the bowl. Stir gently. Slowly add the hot coffee and stir until the flames disappear.

TO SERVE

Add the Cointreau and serve in small warm cups.

Chocolaccino

INGREDIENTS

SERVES 1

¼ cup/50 ml/2 fl oz hot milk

¼ cup/50 ml/2 fl oz hot Italian coffee

TO SERVE

2 tbsp/30 ml double (heavy) cream, lightly whipped

25 g/1 oz grated semi-sweet chocolate

PREPARATION

☛ If you do not have a *cappuccino* maker froth the hot milk in a blender for approximately one minute. Mix with the hot coffee.

TO SERVE

Pour into a tall cup or glass. Spoon over the whipped cream and top with a pile of grated chocolate.

An excellent variation on *Cappuccino!*

Sambuca

Served with coffee beans floating on top, Sambuca carries a hidden message. An odd number of beans is considered lucky whereas an even number is a curse.

Fill a liqueur glass almost to the brim and float the desired number of beans on top. Set alight and after a few seconds gently blow out the blue flames and sip the liqueur. You can, if you wish, crunch a bean after every few sips.

Coffee Noggin

INGREDIENTS

SERVES 6—8

⅔ cup/150 ml/¼ pt milk

⅔ cup/150 ml/¼ pt single (light) cream

1¼ cups/275 ml/½ pt hot sweetened coffee

4 eggs, separated

4 tsp/20 ml Crême de Cacao

⅔ cup/150 ml/¼ pt double (heavy) cream

TO SERVE

grated nutmeg

PREPARATION

☞ Whisk together in a saucepan over a low heat the milk, single cream and sweetened coffee. Do not boil. Whisk in the egg yolks. Cook until the mixture thickens. Strain and cool.

☞ Stir in the Crême de Cacao. Whisk the double cream until it just holds its peaks and fold into the coffee mixture.

☞ Just before serving, whisk the egg whites until stiff and fold into the coffee noggin.

TO SERVE

Serve in glass cups, goblets or mugs. Sprinkle the top with nutmeg.

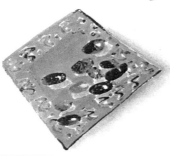

Fruit Coffee Punch

INGREDIENTS

SERVES 8–10

1⅓ cups/225 g/8 oz raspberries

4 oranges

⅔ cup/150 ml/¼ pt Vodka

2½ cups/550 ml/1 pt strong black coffee, cold

TO SERVE

2 bottles sparkling white wine

2 kiwi fruit (Chinese gooseberries)

PREPARATION

☞ Cut the raspberries and slice the oranges. Put straight into the serving or punch bowl. Pour over the Vodka and coffee. Leave to infuse for two hours.

TO SERVE

Add the sparkling white wine and peeled, sliced kiwi fruit. Serve in cups or glasses with the fruit.

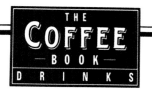
Tropical Coffee Drink

INGREDIENTS

SERVES 4

1 cup/225 g/8 oz mango sorbet (sherbet)

4 tbsp/60 ml Cointreau

½ cup/100 ml/¼ pt cold black coffee

½ cup/100 ml/¼ pt pineapple juice

TO SERVE

8 short straws

PREPARATION

☛ Combine all the ingredients in a blender. Pour into four chilled shallow glasses.

TO SERVE

Serve each one with two straws.

Coffee Crème

INGREDIENTS

SERVES 2

1 cup/225 g/8 fl oz Crème Fraîche

1 cup/225 ml/8 fl oz cold black coffee

2 tbsp/30 ml Crème de Cacao

2 tbsp/30 ml Vodka

TO SERVE

thin ribbon of orange zest

PREPARATION

☛ Put all the ingredients in a blender and pour into chilled tall glasses.

TO SERVE

Decorate with a spiral of orange zest.

Southern Belle

INGREDIENTS

SERVES 2

4 tbsp/60 ml Southern Comfort

4 tbsp/60 ml apricot brandy

1 cup/225 ml/8 fl oz cold black coffee

¼ cup/50 ml/2 fl oz double (heavy) cream

TO SERVE

slices of fresh apricot

PREPARATION

☛ Put all the ingredients into a blender and pour into chilled glasses.

TO SERVE

Decorate with slices of fresh apricot.

Coffee Velvet

INGREDIENTS

SERVES 4

4 tbsp/60 ml Kahlua

1 tbsp/15 ml Crême de Noyaux

1 cup/225 ml/8 fl oz cold black coffee

⅔ cup/175 ml/¼ pt double (heavy) cream

TO SERVE

4 short straws

PREPARATION

☞ Combine all the ingredients in a blender and serve in chilled wide-angled glasses.

TO SERVE

Serve with a short straw.

Coffee Coke Float

INGREDIENTS

SERVES 4

⅔ cup/150 ml/¼ pt single (light) cream

2½ cups/550 ml/1 pt chilled strong sweetened coffee

4 scoops of coffee ice cream

1 large bottle of coca cola

PREPARATION

☛ Stir the cream into the coffee. Mix well. Pour into four tall glasses only half filling. Add a scoop of ice cream to each glass and top up with coca cola.

Iced Coffee and Frappés

When making iced coffee and frappés the rule is the same; you must make good hot coffee to make good iced coffee. Prepare it no more than three hours in advance and chill, covered, in the refrigerator.

Double strength coffee is essential if you are adding lots of ice which will dilute the flavours. Use half the usual amount of water to the same amount of coffee.

Iced Cinnamon Coffee

INGREDIENTS

SERVES 4

2½ cups/550 ml/1 pt hot extra strength black coffee

3 pieces of stick cinnamon

4 cloves

2 tsp/10 g brown sugar

⅔ cup/175 ml/¼ pt single (light) cream

PREPARATION

☛ Pour the coffee over the cinnamon and cloves. Cover and leave to infuse for one hour. Remove the cinnamon and cloves, sweeten to taste. Pour into a liquidizer, add the cream and six ice cubes. Blend to a creamy froth and serve immediately.

Iced Café au Lait

INGREDIENTS

SERVES 4

1¼ cups/275 ml/½ pt hot extra strong coffee

1¼ cups/275 ml/½ pt hot milk

sugar to taste

TO SERVE

4 tbsp/60 ml double (heavy) cream, lightly whipped

PREPARATION

☛ Pour the coffee and milk into a pot. Sweeten to taste. Cover and leave to cool and then refrigerate until cold.

TO SERVE

Pour into four chilled glasses and top with the whipped cream.

Café Mexicano

INGREDIENTS

SERVES 4

¼ cup/50 ml/2 fl oz double (heavy) cream

¾ tsp/4 g cinnamon

¼ tsp/1 g nutmeg

1 tbsp/15 g sugar

2½ cups/550 ml/1 pt double strength hot coffee

4 tsp/20 ml chocolate syrup

PREPARATION

☛ Whip the cream with one-third of the cinnamon, all the nutmeg and sugar. Whip until the cream just holds its peaks.

☛ Put one teaspoon of the chocolate sauce into four demitasse cups. Stir the remaining cinnamon into the coffee and put into the cups. Mix well to blend in the syrup. Spoon over the whipped cream.

Mega Mocha Shake

INGREDIENTS

SERVES 2

3 scoops of coffee ice cream

3 scoops of chocolate ice cream

²/₃ cup/150 ml/¹/₄ pt chilled strong sweetened coffee

²/₃ cup/150 ml/¹/₄ pt milk

TO SERVE

2 long wide straws

2 chocolate flakes (sticks)

PREPARATION

☞ Combine all the ingredients in a blender until creamy.

TO SERVE

Pour out into two chilled tall glasses. Add a wide straw and chocolate flake to each.

Viennese Coffee

What makes this Viennese is the 'Schlagobers' – a large spoonful of sweetened whipped cream as topping.

INGREDIENTS

SERVES 4

½ cup/100 g/4 oz plain chocolate

4 tbsp/60 ml single (light) cream

2½ cups/550 ml/1 pt hot strong coffee

⅔ cup/150 ml/¼ pt double (heavy) cream

1 tsp/5 g sugar

TO SERVE

cinnamon

cocoa

PREPARATION

☛ Gently melt the chocolate in a saucepan taking care not to burn it. Stir in single cream.
☛ Pour in the coffee a little at a time, beating well until frothy. Keep warm. Whip the double cream with the sugar. Pour the coffee into four warmed cups and spoon on the whipped cream.

TO SERVE

Sprinkle with cinnamon and cocoa.

Savouries

Opposite: Creamy Coffee
Coconut Sauce (*see page 67.*)

Meat and Potato Curry

INGREDIENTS

SERVES 4

4 tbsp/50 g/2 oz butter

1 onion, finely chopped

1 clove garlic, crushed

1 tbsp/15 g mild curry paste

1 tbsp/15 g tomato paste

a pinch of salt

3 cups/450 g/1 lb mutton, cubed

1¼ cups/275 ml/½ pt strong black coffee

juice and grated rind of 1 lime

4 cups/450 g/1 lb raw potatoes, cubed

TO SERVE

2 tbsp/30 g fresh coriander, chopped

PREPARATION

☞ Melt the butter in a deep frying pan and fry the onion and garlic for a few minutes.
☞ Stir in the curry paste, tomato paste, salt, mutton, coffee and lime. Bring to the boil and simmer for ¾ hour stirring occasionally. Add the potatoes and continue cooking until tender.

TO SERVE

Garnish with coriander and serve with saffron or turmeric rice.

Creamy Coffee Coconut Sauce

INGREDIENTS

SERVES 4

1½ cups/350 g/12 oz onions, finely chopped

2 cloves garlic, crushed

¼ cup/50 g/2 oz vegetable ghee

3 tbsp/45 ml cooking oil

¾ cup/175 g/6 oz creamed coconut

1¼ cups/275 ml/½ pt hot strong coffee

1 tbsp/15 g garam masala

2 cups/225 g/8 oz red pepper, thinly sliced

PREPARATION

☛ Gently fry the onions and garlic in the ghee and oil until soft and slightly golden.

☛ Chop the creamed coconut in a bowl. Pour over the hot coffee until just covered. Leave to soften slightly and stir until dissolved.

☛ Mix the garam masala with the onion mixture. Cook for 2 to 3 minutes and add the red pepper. Cover and continue cooking for about 5 to 8 minutes until the pepper softens.

☛ Pour in the coconut cream and season to taste with salt. Heat, but do not boil until the sauce thickens.

☛ Serve separately or spooned over curry.

Coffee Chicken Salad

INGREDIENTS

SERVES 4—6

1.5 kg/3 lb (4–6) boneless chicken breasts

1¼ cups/275 ml/½ pt Crème Fraîche

2 tbsp/30 ml coffee essence

2 tbsp/30 g soft brown sugar

⅔ cup/150 ml/¼ pt mayonnaise

6 celery sticks cut into 2.5 cm/1 in strips

1½ cups/175 g/6 oz shelled walnuts

salt and freshly ground black pepper

oven temperature 180°C/350°F/Gas 4

PREPARATION

☛ Cut the chicken breasts into bite size pieces and arrange in one layer in an ovenproof dish. Mix together the Crème Fraîche, coffee essence and brown sugar and spread over the chicken breasts. Bake for 25 to 30 minutes, remove and cool.

☛ Transfer to a serving bowl. Stir the mayonnaise into the mixture and add the celery, walnuts and seasoning. Toss well.

☛ Cover and refrigerate for at least 4 hours. Taste and adjust seasoning before serving.

Coffee Savoury Pancakes

INGREDIENTS

SERVES 4—6

PANCAKES

1 cup/2 tbsp/100 g/4 oz plain (all-purpose) flour

a pinch of salt

1 egg

1¼ cups/275 ml/½ pt strong milky coffee

1 tbsp/15 ml coffee essence

oil for frying

FILLING

1 tbsp/15 ml olive oil

1 small onion, finely chopped

2 cloves garlic, crushed

6 courgettes (zucchini), grated

6 tomatoes, peeled, seeded and chopped

3 tbsp/45 g natural yoghurt (yogurt)

1 tsp/5 g chopped fresh mint

1 cup/100 g/4 oz grated cheddar

PREPARATION

☛ Combine the flour and salt into a bowl. Mix in the egg, add the coffee and coffee essence. Beat until smooth. Leave to stand in the refrigerator for 20 to 30 minutes. Beat again just before using.

☛ Brush the omelette pan with a little oil and heat over a high heat. Pour in one tablespoon of batter, swirl it around until it forms a wafer-thin layer over the pan. Cook for 1½ minutes. Flip over and cook until golden brown. Repeat. Stack the pancakes and keep warm.

☛ Heat the olive oil and gently fry the onions and garlic until the onions are soft and transparent. Stir in the grated courgette and tomatoes. Cook for 6 to 8 minutes, stir in the yoghurt and mint. Season to taste.

☛ Place a generous spoonful of this filling in each pancake, roll up neatly and arrange in a lightly greased, shallow baking dish.

☛ Sprinkle the grated cheese over the pancakes. Place under a hot grill (broiler) until the cheese is melted and serve immediately.

Chicken Casserole

INGREDIENTS

SERVES 6

2 large pinches of salt

2 large pinches of pepper

good ½ cup/50 g/2 oz plain (all-purpose) flour

6 chicken breasts

2 tbsp/30 ml oil

4 tbsp/50 g/2 oz unsalted (sweet) butter

1 cup/225 ml/8 fl oz white wine

1 cup/225 ml/8 fl oz black coffee

8 spring onions (scallions) cut in 2.5 cm/1 in diagonal lengths

4 carrots, sliced thinly

4 courgettes (zucchini) cut into strips

grated rind and juice of 1 lemon

1 tsp/5 g cinnamon

PREPARATION

☞ Season the flour and use it to coat the chicken. Heat the oil and butter and gently fry the chicken until golden brown, remove from the pan.

☞ Add the remaining flour to the pan, the wine and coffee and bring to the boil, stirring all the time.

☞ Return the chicken pieces to the pan and add the vegetables, lemon rind, juice and cinnamon.

☞ Cover and simmer for 30 minutes until the chicken and vegetables are tender.

Baked Beans

INGREDIENTS

SERVES 6

2 cups/450 g/1 lb dried haricot (navy) beans, soaked in cold water overnight

2 tbsp/25 g/1 oz butter

3 cups/450 g/1 lb salt pork cut into cubes

2 onions, finely chopped

2 garlic cloves, crushed

4 small leeks, sliced

1 cup/100 g/4 oz carrots, chopped

4 raw potatoes, washed and cubed

¾ cup/175 ml/¼ pt tomato juice

⅔ cup/150 ml/¼ pt red wine

1¼ cups/275 ml/½ pt strong black coffee

oven temperature 180°C/350°F/Gas 4

PREPARATION

☞ Melt the butter and add the pork, onions and garlic. Cook gently until the onion is soft and transparent. Season to taste.

☞ Put the beans in a large casserole, add the pork and onion mixture and stir in the leeks, carrots, potatoes, tomato juice, red wine and coffee. Mix well. Place the covered casserole in the oven and bake for 2½ to 3 hours until the beans are tender and most of the liquid absorbed. If the beans are still firm and all the liquid has been absorbed, add extra coffee and continue to cook until tender.

☞ Check the seasoning and serve hot with fresh crusty bread.

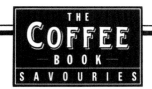
Stuffed Beef Rolls

INGREDIENTS

SERVES 6

12 medium slices of sirloin beef 0.6 cm/¼ in thick

12 thin slices parma ham

3 cloves garlic, crushed

6 spring onions (scallions), chopped

2 cups/350 g/12 oz ricotta cheese

⅔ cup/100 g/4 oz sultanas (white raisins)

8 tbsp/120 g chopped fresh mixed herbs
eg parsley, basil, oregano

salt and freshly ground black pepper

½ tsp/2 g ground nutmeg

1¼ cups/275 ml/½ pt strong black coffee

1¼ cups/275 ml/½ pt dry white wine

2 tbsp/30 ml coffee liqueur

oven temperature 190°C/375°F/Gas 5

PREPARATION

☛ Flatten the sliced beef.

☛ Place a slice of ham onto each slice of beef. Mix together in a bowl the garlic, spring onions, ricotta cheese, sultanas, chopped herbs, salt and pepper and nutmeg. Spoon this mixture onto each of the beef slices and roll up. Secure with fine string. Put the rolls into an ovenproof dish and pour over the coffee and wine. Bake for 20 minutes. Add the coffee liqueur and bake for a further 20 to 30 minutes.

☛ Serve with hot buttered noodles.

Coffee Spareribs

INGREDIENTS

SERVES 6

6 pork sparerib chops cut into individual ribs

3 tbsp/45 ml olive oil

2 cloves garlic, crushed

2 tbsp/30 g parsley, chopped

2/3 cup/150 ml/1/4 pt red wine

2/3 cup/150 ml/1/4 pt strong black coffee

3 tbsp/45 ml honey

salt and freshly ground black pepper

grated rind and juice of 1 lime

oven temperature 180°C/350°F/Gas 4

PREPARATION

☛ Place the spareribs in a large shallow pan. Mix all the remaining ingredients together and pour over the spareribs. Leave to marinate overnight, turning occasionally.

☛ Remove the ribs from the marinade. Place under a pre-heated grill (broiler), turning until evenly browned. Place ribs back into the marinade and bake for 30 minutes.

☛ Remove the ribs and skim the fat off the sauce.

☛ Serve with rice.

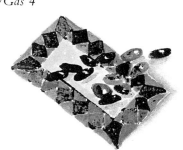

Crumbly Veal Escalopes

INGREDIENTS

SERVES 4

4 slices veal fillet

2¼ cups/175 g/6 oz brown dried breadcrumbs

2 tbsp/30 g medium ground coffee

2 tbsp/30 g light brown sugar

grated rind of two oranges

salt and pepper

2 eggs, beaten

4 tbsp/50 g/2 oz unsalted (sweet) butter

2 tbsp/30 ml oil

SAUCE

2 tbsp/25 g/1 oz unsalted (sweet) butter

4 tbsp/25 g/1 oz plain (all-purpose) flour

⅔ cup/150 ml/¼ pt strong black coffee

⅔ cup/150 ml/¼ pt milk

1 tbsp/15 ml coffee liqueur

TO SERVE

orange segments and watercress sprigs

PREPARATION

☛ Dry the slices of veal thoroughly. Place each one between sheets of greaseproof (waxed) paper. Beat firmly with a rolling pin or mallet to flatten the meat but not too heavily as this will tear the meat. Flatten to a thickness of 6 mm/¼ in.

☛ Mix together the breadcrumbs, coffee, sugar, orange rind, salt and freshly ground black pepper. Dip the escalopes into the egg and then into the breadcrumb mixture to coat lightly.

☛ Heat the butter and oil in a large frying pan over a moderate to high heat. When the foam has subsided add the escalopes in one layer. Adding more butter and oil as required, fry for 4 to 5 minutes on each side, keeping the fat hot but not burning.

☛ Remove the escalopes and place in a hot serving dish. Keep warm while the sauce is being made.

☛ Put all the other ingredients, except the liqueur, into a saucepan and heat. Whisking continuously, cook until smooth and shiny. Stir in the coffee liqueur. Pour the sauce over the veal escalopes.

TO SERVE

Garnish with the orange and watercress sprigs.

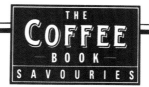
Lamb Extravaganza

INGREDIENTS

SERVES 4–6

450 g/1 lb lamb fillet

3 tbsp/45 g paprika

2 tbsp/30 g chilli (chili) powder

2 tbsp/30 g fresh coriander, chopped

2 tbsp/30 g fresh parsley, chopped

6 tbsp/75 ml Crème Fraîche

3 tbsp/45 ml oil

2 cloves garlic

1 onion finely chopped

2 cups/100 g/4 oz mushrooms, sliced

1 red pepper, seeded and sliced

about 2 cups/450 ml/16 oz pineapple slices
in own juice, quartered

1¼ cups/275 ml/½ pt strong black coffee

4 tsp/20 g cornflour (cornstarch)/water to mix

TO SERVE

lime and coriander to garnish

PREPARATION

☛ Cut the meat into 2.5 cm/1 in cubes. Mix together the paprika, chilli, coriander, parsley and Crème Fraîche in a bowl. Coat the meat with this mixture.

☛ Heat the oil in a deep frying pan and lightly fry the garlic and vegetables for 2 to 3 minutes. Drain. Cook the meat for 10 minutes stirring occasionally, and mix in the vegetables.

☛ Add the pineapple and coffee and simmer for 10 to 15 minutes. Blend the cornflour with cold water and add to the pan. Stir until the sauce thickens. Adjust the seasoning.

TO SERVE

Garnish with slices of lime and sprigs of coriander. Serve with brown rice.

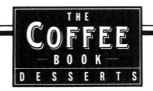

Desserts

Opposite: Cocoa Rica (*see page 78.*)

Cocoa Rica

INGREDIENTS

SERVES 6

2 tbsp/12 g/½ oz powdered gelatine (gelatin)

4 tbsp/60 ml water

2 tbsp/25 g/1 oz sugar

⅓ cup/75 ml/3 fl oz strong black Italian coffee

¼ cup/50 ml/2 fl oz coffee liqueur

1¼ cups/275 ml/½ pt double (heavy) cream

TO SERVE

crystallized violets

PREPARATION

☛ Melt the gelatine in a bowl of water, over a pan of simmering water. Remove from heat and, when cool and beginning to thicken, add the sugar, coffee and liqueur.

☛ Whisk the cream until soft and gradually add the coffee mixture to the cream. Continue whisking until the cream is thick and beginning to set.

☛ Pour the cream into serving glasses and chill for 2 to 3 hours.

TO SERVE

Before serving, decorate each glass with crystallized violets.

Gilded Coffee Pears

INGREDIENTS

SERVES 4

4 dessert pears (with stalks)

1¼ cups/275 ml/½ pt strong black coffee

⅔ cup/150 ml/¼ pt sweet white wine

1½ cups/225 g/8 oz raspberries

⅔ cup/150 ml/¼ pt good sauterne

icing (confectioner's) sugar

TO SERVE

4 mint sprigs

gold edible food colouring in powder form (optional)

PREPARATION

☛ Peel the pears thinly leaving the stalk intact (if necessary cut a sliver off the base so that the pears stand upright). Poach the pears in the coffee and sweet white wine for 20 to 30 minutes according to the variety and ripeness of the fruit.

☛ When cooked but still firm to touch, remove from the liquid and cool. Put the raspberries and sauterne wine into a saucepan and heat gently until the raspberries are soft. Stir well to break up the berries and strain. Cool and chill the sauce, sweeten to taste with the icing sugar.

☛ Either arrange the pears on a serving plate and spoon the sauce over, or place on individual plates and spoon a little of the sauce onto and around the pear. Serve the remaining sauce separately.

TO SERVE

Decorate each pear with a sprig of mint.

Lightly dust the pear stalks and the edges of the mint sprigs with the gold food colour.

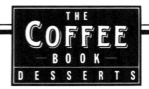

Cappuccino Ice

A smooth, mellow version of the Granita al Caffé.

INGREDIENTS

SERVES 6—10

2 cups/450 ml/¾ pt strong Italian coffee

¾ cup/175 ml/¼ pt whipping cream

½ cup/100 g/4 oz granulated sugar

PREPARATION

☛ Pour all ingredients into a saucepan and heat gently. Stir continuously until the sugar dissolves and the mixture comes to the boil. Allow the mixture to cool to about 100°F/38°C in temperature. Then transfer to a shallow dish and place in freezer.

☛ Allow mixture to freeze solid which will take 3 to 6 hours.

☛ Before serving put in the refrigerator for 30 minutes.

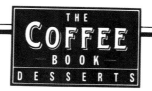

Austrian Coffee Pudding

INGREDIENTS

oven temperature 200°C/400°F/Gas 6

PASTRY

1 tsp/5 g dried yeast
3 tbsp/45 g lukewarm milk
2½ cups/250 g/9 oz plain (all-purpose) flour
3 tbsp/45 ml cooking oil
4 tbsp/50 g/2 oz butter, melted
1 egg
2 tbsp/30 g instant coffee, dissolved in 1 tbsp/15 ml hot water
2 tbsp/25 g/1 oz sugar

DECORATION

½ cup/100 g/4 oz butter
1 cup + 2 tbsp/100 g/4 oz plain (all-purpose) flour
bare 1 cup/200 g/7 oz sugar
2 tbsp/25 g/1 oz vanilla sugar
⅓ cup/75 g/3 oz ground almonds
2 tbsp/30 ml coffee liqueur
450 g/1 lb ripe apricots, halved and stoned

PREPARATION

☛ Dissolve the yeast in the milk. Put the flour into a bowl, making a well in the centre and pour in the oil, butter, lukewarm yeast liquid, egg, coffee and sugar.

☛ Mix all the ingredients together to form a dough. Knead lightly, cover and leave to stand in a warm place for 1 hour.

☛ To decorate, rub the butter into the flour until the mixture resembles breadcrumbs. Stir in the sugars and ground almonds. Mix well.

☛ Knead the dough lightly and press into the base of a well greased 20 cm/8 in loose-bottomed cake pan. Cover with apricot halves, which have been soaked in coffee liqueur for 30 minutes, and breadcrumb mix. Cook for 30 to 40 minutes.

Paris-Brest

This dessert was created to celebrate a famous bicycle race from Paris to Brest and back again. A delicious variation of a classic recipe!

INGREDIENTS

SERVES 6–8

CHOUX PASTRY

⅔ cup/150 ml/¼ pt water

4 tbsp/50 g/2 oz unsalted (sweet) butter

⅔ cup/65 g/2½ oz plain (all-purpose) flour

pinch of salt

2 eggs beaten

⅓ cup/40 g/1½ oz flaked almonds

FILLING

450 g/1 lb cherries, stoned and marinated overnight in kirsch

1¼ cups/275 ml/½ pt double (heavy) cream

3 tbsp/45 g icing (confectioner's) sugar

2 tbsp/30 g instant coffee dissolved in 1 tbsp/15 ml hot water

oven temperature 200°C/400°F/Gas 6

PREPARATION

☞ Heat the water and butter in a saucepan until the butter melts and the water boils. Remove from the heat and quickly beat in the flour and salt. Continue beating over a low heat until the paste is smooth and leaves the sides of the pan clean.

☞ Remove from the heat and add the eggs a little at a time, beating well between each addition until the mixture is smooth and shiny.

☞ Spoon the mixture into a piping (pastry) bag fitted with a plain 2.5 cm/1 in nozzle. Pipe a circle about 3.8 cm/1½ in wide and 20.3 cm/8 in in diameter on a greased baking tray. Sprinkle the almonds evenly over the dough and bake for 30 minutes. Remove from the oven and slice through the middle with a sharp knife. Cool both halves separately.

☞ Place the pastry base onto a serving plate. Spoon the drained cherries into the bottom half of the ring. Whip together the cream, sugar and coffee, and spoon onto the cherries.

☞ Cover with the top of the pastry and dust with icing (confectioner's) sugar.

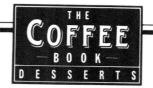

Coffee Pear Tart

INGREDIENTS

SERVES 10

PASTRY

¾ cup/150 g/6 oz butter

3½ cups/350 g/12 oz plain (all-purpose) flour

1 tbsp/15 g sugar

2 tbsp/30 g powdered instant coffee dissolved
in 1 tbsp/15 ml warm water

1 egg

FILLING

1 kg/2 lb firm ripe pears

2 eggs beaten

6 tbsp/75 ml double (heavy) cream

2 tbsp/30 g powdered instant coffee dissolved
in 1 tbsp/15 ml warm water

1 liqueur glass of coffee liqueur

oven temperature 200°C/400°F/Gas 6

PREPARATION

☛ Rub the butter into the flour and stir in the sugar. Mix together the coffee and egg and use to bind the mixture together. If more liquid is required use water. Roll out the pastry and line a 30 cm/12 in loose-bottom flan tin (pie plate). Bake for 15 minutes.

☛ Peel, halve and core the pears and arrange in a circle in the pastry case (pie shell).

☛ Mix together the eggs, cream, coffee and liqueur. Pour over the pears and bake for 30 minutes. Serve warm.

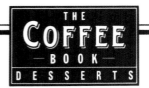
Tropical Coffee Slice

STAGE ONE

STAGE TWO

INGREDIENTS

SERVES 8
4 egg whites
1 cup/225 g/8 oz sugar
2 tbsp/30 g powdered instant coffee
⅔ cup/75 g/3 oz ground almonds
¼ cup/25 g/1 oz flaked toasted almonds
⅔ cup/150 ml/¼ pt double (heavy) cream
1 small fresh pineapple, peeled, cored and chopped into pieces
½ cup/50 g/2 oz desiccated (shredded) coconut

oven temperature 100°C/200°F/Gas

PREPARATION

☛ Draw two rectangles 30.5 cm × 10 cm/12 in × 4 in onto sheets of nonstick (waxed) paper. Place up-side down on baking sheets.

☛ Beat the egg whites until stiff and whisk in 4 tbsp/60 g of sugar and the coffee. Continue whisking until the meringue forms stiff peaks. Fold in the remaining sugar and ground almonds.

☛ Spoon the meringue into a piping (pastry) bag fitted with a 1 cm/½ in plain nozzle. Pipe in lines across the width of each rectangle. Sprinkle one rectangle with the toasted almonds. Bake for 2 hours and leave to cool.

☛ Whip the cream until thick and soft, spread over the meringue base without almonds. Cover with the pineapple pieces and sprinkle over the coconut. Top with the second meringue layer. Refrigerate for 2 hours.

Coffee Cheesecake

INGREDIENTS

SERVES 10–12

BASE

½ cup/100 g/4 oz butter

½ cup/100 g/4 oz dark brown sugar

2 cups/225 g/8 oz coffee biscuits, crushed

FILLING

¼ cup/25 g/1 oz powdered gelatine (gelatin)

6 tbsp/75 ml warm water

2 cups/450 g/1 lb cream cheese

4 eggs, separated

1 cup/225 g/8 oz dark brown sugar

2 tbsp/30 g powdered instant coffee dissolved in 1 tbsp/15 ml hot water

1¼ cups/275 ml/½ pt double (heavy) cream

TO SERVE

crystallized rose petals

PREPARATION

☛ Grease a 25–10 cm/10–12 in loose-bottomed cake pan. Melt the butter in a saucepan. Stir in the sugar and biscuits. Spoon into the pan and press down firmly with the back of a spoon. Chill.

☛ Dissolve the gelatine in a bowl of warm water over a pan of simmering water. Beat the cream cheese in a bowl until soft and beat in the egg yolks, half the sugar, coffee and cream. Stir well. Dissolve the gelatine in the warm water and add to the coffee mixture. Leave the mixture until it is on the point of setting.

☛ Whisk the egg whites until stiff and whisk in the remaining sugar. Gently fold into the coffee mixture. Pour into the chilled biscuit base. Gently tilt and tip the pan to level the surface.

☛ Chill for 3–4 hours.

☛ Run a heated palette knife (metal spatula) around the edge of the cheesecake and remove from pan.

TO SERVE

Transfer to a serving plate and decorate the top with the crystallized rose petals.

Steamed Coffee Pudding

INGREDIENTS

SERVES 6

2½ cups/125 g/5 oz dry coffee sponge cake

⅓ cup/75 g/3 oz plain chocolate

⅔ cup/150 ml/¼ pt milky coffee

4 tbsp/50 g/2 oz butter

2 tbsp/30 g vanilla sugar

2 large eggs, separated

2 tbsp/30 g powdered instant coffee dissolved
in 1 tbsp/15 ml hot water

PREPARATION

☛ Crumble the cake into fine crumbs. Melt the chocolate in a bowl over a pan of hot, gently simmering, water. When melted, pour over the cake crumbs. Leave to stand for 30 minutes.

☛ Cream the butter and sugar together until light and fluffy; beat in the egg yolks. Stir in the soaked crumbs and coffee.

☛ Beat the egg whites until stiff and gently fold into the chocolate and coffee mixture. Spoon into a large buttered pudding bowl – the mixture should only half fill it. Cover with greased foil or double thickness of greaseproof (waxed) paper. Place in a steamer and steam for 1½ hours. Turn out the pudding onto a serving dish, dust with sugar and serve with custard, cream or chocolate sauce.

Coffee Charlotte

INGREDIENTS

SERVES 6

32 sponge fingers (lady fingers)

4 tbsp/60 ml water

4 tbsp/60 ml coffee liqueur

1 cup/225 ml/8 fl oz milky coffee

¼ cup/50 g/2 oz vanilla sugar

4 tbsp/25 g/1 oz plain (all-purpose) flour

⅓ cup/50 g/2 oz ground almonds

1 whole egg

1 egg yolk

1 cup/100 g/4 oz coarsely grated milk chocolate

PREPARATION

☛ Dip the sponge fingers lightly in the mixture of water and liqueur, and line the base and sides of a 15–18 cm/6–7 in charlotte mould (mold).

☛ Heat the milky coffee. Mix the sugar, flour and ground almonds together. Add the eggs and gradually pour over the coffee in the saucepan, beating thoroughly. Bring to the boil stirring constantly. Remove from the heat and leave to cool. Spoon a layer of the coffee cream into the mould and sprinkle over a layer of grated chocolate. Repeat until all the cream is used. Trim the sponge fingers lining the mould level with the filling and arrange the trimmings on top.

☛ Press down well and leave to stand for 4 to 6 hours in a refrigerator until firm.

Coffee Coconut Soufflé

INGREDIENTS

SERVES 4—6

3 eggs, separated

4 tbsp/60 ml strong black coffee

1 tbsp/15 ml Crême de Curaçao

⅓ cup/75 g/3 oz sugar

½ cup/50 g/2½ oz desiccated (shredded) coconut

2 tbsp/15 g/½ oz powdered gelatine (gelatin)

2 tbsp/30 ml cold water

⅔ cup/150 ml/¼ pt double (heavy) cream

PREPARATION

☛ Beat the egg yolks, coffee, Crême de Curaçao, and sugar in a bowl until thick. Stir in most of the coconut. Melt the gelatine in a bowl of water over a pan of hot water. When clear, pour slowly into the coffee mixture, stirring all the time.

☛ Beat the cream until it just holds its shape and fold into the mixture. Whisk the egg whites until nearly stiff and fold them carefully into the mixture when nearly set.

☛ Prepare a soufflé dish by cutting a band of paper 7.6 cm/3 in deeper than the dish from a double layer of nonstick (waxed) paper. Fold up 2.5 cm/1 in along one of the long edges. Wrap the band round the dish, the folded edge level with the base and the upper edge extending beyond the rim by 5 cm/2 in. Secure firmly with string or paper clips. Spoon the mixture into the dish until it almost reaches the top of the paper band. Remove the paper and decorate with remaining shredded (desiccated) coconut.

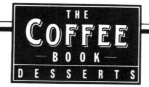
Coffee Brulée

INGREDIENTS

SERVES 6

3 cups/675 ml/1¼ pt single (table) cream

6 egg yolks

1 tbsp/15 g vanilla sugar

1½ tbsp/22 ml vanilla essence (extract)

4 tbsp/60 g instant powdered coffee

2 tbsp/30 g coffee liqueur

2 tbsp/30 g Demerara sugar

oven temperature 150°C/300°F/Gas 2

PREPARATION

☛ Place the cream in a bowl over a pan of simmering water. Beat the egg yolks, add the vanilla sugar and essence, coffee and liqueur and gently stir into the warmed cream. Continue cooking, stirring all the time, until the sauce is thick enough to coat the back of the wooden spoon.

☛ Strain the cream through a fine sieve into either a large soufflé dish or individual custard dishes.

☛ Put the dish or dishes into a large shallow dish and place on the middle rack of the oven. Fill oven dish with hot water until it reaches the level of the custard in the serving dishes. Bake for 35 to 45 minutes until the centre of the custard is firm.

☛ Remove the custard dishes from the water. Cool, cover and chill. Sift the Demerara sugar on top of the chilled custard. Place under a preheated hot grill (broiler) as close to the heat as possible.

☛ Grill (broil) until the sugar has caramelized. Watch closely.

☛ Remove and chill for 2 to 3 hours.

Coffee and Raspberry Frou Frou

INGREDIENTS

SERVES 6–8

2½ cups/550 ml/1 pt double (heavy) cream

2½ cups/550 ml/1 pt single (light) cream

2 cups/225 g/8 oz cooked meringues

4 tsp/20 g powdered instant coffee dissolved
in 1 tbsp/15 ml hot water, cooled

1 cup/100 g/4 oz frozen or fresh raspberries

1 tsp/5 ml lemon juice

3 tbsp/35 g/1½ oz vanilla sugar

grated rind of one orange

1 tbsp/15 ml water

a selection of mixed fruit washed and sliced
e.g. strawberries, raspberries, peaches

PREPARATION

☛ Whip the two creams together until they just hold in soft peaks. Break the meringue into small pieces and fold into the cream. Divide the mixture between three bowls. Add the coffee to one bowl and fold in.

☛ For the raspberry sauce, combine all the remaining ingredients, except the mixed fruit, in a saucepan and heat gently until the raspberries are soft. Stir well to break up the berries and mix with one of the bowls of cream and meringue mixture. Grease a 1.75 l/3 pt ring mould (mold) and alternate spoonfuls of the mixtures from the 3 bowls into the mould. Repeat until all the mixture is used. Gently smooth the surface and cover. Freeze for at least 6 hours.

☛ Place in a refrigerator 30 minutes before serving as this makes unmoulding easier.

☛ Place on serving plate and fill the centre with the mixed fruit.

Luxury Mocha Ice Cream

INGREDIENTS

2/3 cup/125 g/5 oz plain chocolate

4 eggs, separated

4 tbsp/60 g strong coffee

1¼ cups/275 ml/½ pt double (heavy) cream

1 tbsp/15 ml coffee liqueur

½ cup/100 g/4 oz sugar

TO SERVE

chocolate curls

PREPARATION

☛ Place the chocolate in a bowl over a pan of hot water. When melted, remove from the heat and beat in the egg yolks and coffee.

☛ In a large bowl, whip the cream until stiff and fold in the coffee liqueur.

☛ In another bowl whisk the egg whites until they form stiff peaks, gradually adding the sugar.

☛ Whisk the mocha mixture into the cream and then fold it gently into the egg whites.

☛ Spoon into a 1.75 l/3 pt freeze-proof container. Freeze for at least 5 hours. It is not necessary to stir the ice cream during the freezing time. This ice cream is quite soft so you can serve straight from the freezer.

TO SERVE

Scoop into sundae glasses and decorate with chocolate curls.

An alternative serving suggestion is to scoop the ice cream into individual biscuit base (cookie crumb) tartlets.

Coffee Praline Mousse

INGREDIENTS

SERVES 6

¾ cup/100 g/4 oz whole hazelnuts (filberts)

3 tbsp/45 g sugar

4 large eggs, separated

6 tbsp/75 g vanilla sugar

2 tbsp/30 g powdered instant coffee

1¼ cups/275 ml/½ pt double (heavy) cream

PREPARATION

☛ Brown the hazelnuts in a frying pan over a medium heat. When the skins begin to loosen, remove from heat. Place in a dish cloth and rub gently to remove the skins. Chop roughly. Add the sugar to the pan. When the sugar has melted and is slightly brown, stir in the hazelnuts (filberts). Pour the mixture onto a lightly oiled tray. When cool, break the praline into pieces and blend briefly in a blender.

☛ Beat the egg yolks with 4 tbsp/60 g of vanilla sugar until pale and light. Place the bowl over a pan of hot water and continue beating until the mixture leaves a trail. Stir in the coffee and allow to cool.

☛ Whip the cream in a bowl until soft peaks form and gently stir in the coffee mixture. Fold in the praline. Whisk the egg whites until stiff and beat in the remaining sugar. Gently fold the egg whites into the cream mixture.

☛ Pour the mixture either into a glass serving bowl or individual glasses.

☛ Cover and freeze for at least 1 to 2 hours.

☛ Remove from the freezer 20 minutes before serving.

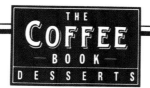

Coffee Bread Pudding

INGREDIENTS

SERVES 6

20 slices day old bread (crusts removed)

1¼ cups/275 ml/½ pt orange juice

1¼ cups/275 ml/½ pt strong black coffee

2 large eggs

¼ cup/50 g/2 oz sugar

½ cup/75 g/3 oz sultanas (white raisins)

¾ cup/75 g/3 oz candied orange peel

½ cup/100 ml/¼ pt Tia Maria

1 tsp/5 g ground cinnamon

1 tsp/5 g ground allspice

butter for greasing

2 tbsp/25 g/1 oz butter

oven temperature 170°C/325°F/Gas 3

PREPARATION

☛ Soak the bread in orange juice and coffee, and mash to a pulp.

☛ Beat the egg yolks and add them to the mashed bread. Stir in the sugar, sultanas, orange peel, Tia Maria and spices.

☛ Whisk the egg whites until they form stiff peaks and fold into the mixture.

☛ Butter a 1.5 l/3 pt ovenproof dish, pour the mixture into it and cover with knobs of butter.

☛ Bake for 30 minutes until golden brown.

Coffee Apricot Condé

INGREDIENTS

SERVES 8

½ cup/100 g/4 oz short-grain rice

5 cups/1½ pt milk

4 tbsp/60 g powdered instant coffee

2 tbsp/15 g/½ oz powdered gelatine (gelatin)

juice of 1 orange

4 tbsp/60 g sugar

⅔ cup/150 ml/¼ pt double (heavy) cream, whipped

4 apricots, peeled, stoned and chopped

1 cup/100 g/4 oz raspberries

⅔ cup/150 ml/¼ pt double (heavy) cream, whipped

4 apricots, stoned and sliced thickly

PREPARATION

☛ Put the rice, milk and coffee into a pan and bring to the boil, stirring occasionally. Simmer for 30 to 40 minutes, or until the rice is cooked, adding extra milk if necessary. Dissolve the gelatine in the orange juice over a pan of hot water. Stir into the rice mixture and add the sugar. Leave to cool.

☛ When cool fold the cream and chopped apricots into the rice mixture. Spoon into a greased 2 qt/ 1.1 1/2 pt mould (mold). Chill until set.

☛ Turn out onto a serving plate, arrange some raspberries around the base, pipe the whipped cream onto the top of the mould and decorate with the rest of the raspberries and apricot slices.

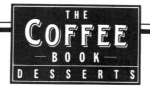

Coffee Meringue Pyramid

INGREDIENTS

SERVES 8—10

8 egg whites

4 tbsp/60 g instant coffee powder

2 cups/450 g/1 lb sugar

2½ cups/550 ml/1 pt double (heavy) cream, whipped

¾ cup/225 g/8 oz black grapes, halved and seeded

¾ cup/225 g/8 oz green grapes, halved and seeded

⅔ cup/100 g/4 oz flaked almonds

chocolate coffee beans

oven temperature 120°C/250°F/Gas ¼

PREPARATION

☛ Line a baking tray with non-stick (waxed) paper. Whisk the egg whites until they form very stiff peaks. Mix the coffee with the sugar and add a little at a time, beating well after each addition.

☛ Place the mixture in a piping (pastry) bag fitted with a star nozzle and pipe small meringues 2.5 cm/ 1 in in diameter onto the non-stick paper.

☛ Bake for 2 to 3 hours until crisp and dry.

☛ To serve place a layer of meringues closely together on a plate and cover with some of the cream, grapes and almonds. Continue with layers of meringue, cream and grapes to form a pyramid.

☛ Decorate with almonds, cream, grapes and chocolate coffee beans.

Mocha Bombe

INGREDIENTS

SERVES 6−8

CREAM LAYER

2 cups/450 ml/¾ pt whipping cream

2 tbsp/25 g/1 oz vanilla sugar

2 tbsp/25 g/1 oz vanilla essence (extract)

MOCHA FILLING

1 full quantity of Luxury Mocha Ice
Cream (see recipe page 91)

COFFEE CREAM

2 cups/450 ml/¾ pt whipping cream

1½ tsp/7 g instant powdered coffee dissolved in 1 tbsp/
15 ml hot water

1 tbsp/15 g vanilla sugar

⅓ cup/50 g/2 oz toasted almonds

PREPARATION

☛ Chill a 2 qt/2 l/3½ pt pudding bowl or bombe mould (mold). Whisk the cream, sugar and essence together until stiff, then spread in the pudding basin to line it evenly. Freeze until firm.

☛ Pour the luxury mocha ice cream into the cream lined basin, cover and freeze for 24 hours.

☛ To serve place the bowl briefly into a larger bowl of hot water then turn out onto a large serving plate.

☛ Whisk the cream, instant coffee and sugar until firm. Pipe a decoration over the bombe and decorate with the toasted almonds.

☛ Return to the freezer until hard, and serve.

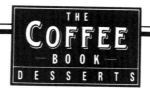

Coffee and Vanilla Jelly

INGREDIENTS

SERVES 6

COFFEE

2 tbsp/25 g/1 oz vanilla sugar

1¼ cups/275 ml/½ pt hot strong coffee

2 tbsp/12 g/½ oz powdered gelatine (gelatin)

3 tbsp/45 ml water

VANILLA

1 egg yolk

2 tbsp/25 g/1 oz vanilla sugar

1¼ cups/275 ml/½ pt milk

vanilla essence (extract)

2 tbsp/12 g/½ oz powdered gelatine (gelatin)

3 tbsp/45 ml water

PREPARATION

☛ Add the vanilla sugar to the hot coffee. Dissolve the gelatine in the water over a saucepan of hot water. Add to the coffee mixture and stir well to make sure the jelly is clear. Pour half the mixture into a greased 1 qt/¾ l/1½ pt decorative jelly mould (mold). Leave to set but keep the rest of the mixture warm. Mix the egg yolk with the sugar, pour on the milk in a saucepan and heat, stirring all the time.
☛ When thickened, add the vanilla essence. Strain and cool. Melt the gelatine in the water and add to the vanilla cream. Pour half this mixture onto the set coffee jelly and leave this to set. Repeat the layers.
☛ Refrigerate until completely set and then turn out onto a serving plate.

Baking

Opposite: Coffee Slices (*see page 100.*)

Coffee Slices

INGREDIENTS

MAKES 18

½ cup/100 g/4 oz butter

¼ cup/50 g/2 oz sugar

1 cup + 2 tbsp/100 g/4 oz self-raising (self-rising) flour

1 tbsp/15 ml coffee essence

ICING

4 tbsp/60 g icing (confectioner's) sugar

1 tbsp/15 g instant coffee

4 tbsp/50 g/2 oz butter

oven temperature 180°C/350°F/Gas 4

PREPARATION

☛ Cream together the butter and sugar until light and fluffy. Fold in the flour and coffee essence.

☛ Press into a greased Swiss (jelly) roll pan and bake for 15 to 20 minutes.

☛ Place all the icing ingredients into a saucepan and heat and stir for 2–3 minutes until the mixture looks like fudge.

☛ Pour the mixture on top of the shortbread. Leave to set and cut into slices.

Mocha Hazel Cake

INGREDIENTS

SERVES 6

¾ cup/100 g/4 oz hazelnuts, shelled

3 egg whites

1 tbsp/15 g instant coffee powder

½ cup/100 g/4 oz granulated sugar

1 tsp/5 g white vinegar

4 tbsp/25 g/1 oz grated chocolate

FILLING

½ cup/100 g/4 oz plain black chocolate

2 tbsp/30 ml coffee liqueur

1¼ cups/275 ml/½ pt double (heavy) cream, whipped

½ cup/100 g/4 oz chocolate shavings

oven temperature 100°C/200°F/Gas ¼

PREPARATION

☛ Roast the hazelnuts in a hot oven until well browned. Put inside a dry dish cloth and rub off the skins. Cool and chop roughly.

☛ Whisk the egg whites until they form stiff peaks. Mix the coffee powder and 1 tbsp/15 g sugar and whisk in. Fold in the remaining sugar and vinegar. Lastly, fold in the nuts with 4 tbsp/25g/1 oz grated chocolate.

☛ Line two baking trays with non-stick (waxed) paper. Mark out two 20 cm/8 in circles and spread the mixture out to cover them.

☛ Bake for 1¾ hours until the meringue has dried out. Cool on wire racks.

FILLING

☛ Melt ⅓ cup/75 g/3 oz plain chocolate with the coffee liqueur. Leave until cool but not set.

☛ Fold the chocolate mixture into the cream. Use the filling to sandwich the meringue rounds together. Decorate with the chocolate shavings.

Coffee Carrot Cake

INGREDIENTS

SERVES 8–10

½ cup/100 g/4 oz butter

¾ cup/175 g/6 oz sugar

1 egg

½ tsp/2½ g mixed spice

4 tbsp/60 g marmalade/1 grated orange rind

2 tbsp/30 ml orange juice

4 tbsp/60 ml strong black coffee

2 cups/225 g/8 oz carrots, grated

½ cup/50 g/2 oz walnuts

2¼ cups/225 g/8 oz self-raising (self-rising) flour

TOPPING

½ cup/100 g/4 oz soft cream cheese

4 tbsp/50 g/2 oz unsalted (sweet) butter

⅔ cup/75 g/3 oz icing (confectioner's) sugar

1 tsp/5 ml vanilla essence

juice of ½ lemon

oven temperature 180°C/350°F/Gas 4

PREPARATION

☛ Cream the butter and sugar together until light and fluffy. Beat in the egg, mixed spice, marmalade, orange rind, juice and coffee. Mix well. Toss the carrots and walnuts in the flour and gradually stir them into the beaten mixture.

☛ Line and grease a 20 cm/8 in cake pan.

☛ Bake for 1½ hours.

☛ Cool the cake in the pan for one hour. Remove and finish cooling on a wire rack.

☛ Cream the cream cheese and butter together. Slowly sift in the icing sugar and continue beating until the mixture is quite smooth. Stir in the vanilla and lemon juice.

☛ Spread ⅔ of the mixture on top of the carrot cake. Place the remainder in piping (pastry) bag and pipe rosettes around the cake.

Coffee Swiss Roll

INGREDIENTS

SERVES 8

2 tbsp/25 g/1 oz butter

3 large eggs

⅓ cup/75 g/3 oz sugar

1 tbsp/15 ml coffee essence

¾ cup/75 g/3 oz plain (all-purpose) flour

pinch of salt

1 tbsp/15 ml hot strong coffee

6 tbsp/75 g warmed Morello cherry jam

⅔ cup/150 ml/¼ pt double (heavy) cream

1 tbsp/15 ml coffee liqueur

4 tbsp/25 g/1 oz coarsely grated plain chocolate

oven temperature 210°C/425°F/Gas 7

PREPARATION

☛ Butter a pan 30.5 cm × 20.3 cm/12 in × 8 in and line with buttered greaseproof (waxed) paper or non-stick paper.

☛ Put the eggs, sugar and coffee essence in a large bowl over a pan of hot water and whisk until the mixture is pale and leaves a thick trail.

☛ Remove from heat and sift half the flour and salt over the egg mixture and fold in carefully, using a large metal spoon.

☛ Repeat with the remaining flour and add the hot coffee.

☛ Turn the mixture quickly into the prepared pan, tilting it until evenly covered.

☛ Bake immediately just above the centre of the oven for about 10 minutes or until well risen and springy.

☛ Have ready a sheet of greaseproof (waxed) or non-stick paper drenched with sugar.

☛ Turn the sponge cake out onto the paper and roll up the sponge cake at once from the short side, making the first turn firm, then rolling lightly. Cool on a wire rack covered with a dish cloth and with the join of the sponge cake underneath.

☛ When cold, carefully unroll the sponge cake, remove the lining paper and brush with Morello jam. Whip the cream and liqueur together, spread over the jam and carefully re-roll the sponge cake.

☛ Sprinkle chocolate over the top.

Wholewheat Coffee Bread

INGREDIENTS

1 cup + 2 tbsp/100 g/4 oz plain (all purpose) flour

1 cup + 2 tbsp/100 g/4 oz wholemeal (wholewheat) flour

3 tbsp/35 g/1½ oz Demerara sugar

3 tbsp/35 g/1½ oz sultanas (white raisins)

⅓ cup/35 g/1½ oz chopped mixed peel

2 tbsp/30 ml coffee essence

½ cup/100 g/4 oz butter

½ cup/100 g/4 oz golden syrup

½ cup/100 g/4 oz molasses

1 tsp/5 g bicarbonate of soda (baking soda)

1¼ cups/275 ml/½ pt strong milky coffee

1 egg, beaten

2 tbsp/25 g/1 oz chopped hazelnuts

oven temperature 180°C/350°F/Gas 4

PREPARATION

☛ Mix together the plain flour, wholewheat flour, Demerara sugar, sultanas and mixed peel. In a large pan, melt together the coffee essence, butter, golden syrup and molasses. Add to the flour and beat well.

☛ Dissolve the bicarbonate of soda in the milky coffee and beat in the egg.

☛ Pour into the prepared mixture and beat to form a smooth batter.

☛ Pour the mixture into a greased and lined oblong pan 15 cm × 22.8 cm/6 in × 9 in. Scatter the hazelnuts over the top.

☛ Bake in the centre of a moderate oven for 40 to 45 minutes until well risen and springy to the touch.

☛ Leave to cool for 15 minutes and turn out to cool further on a wire rack. When cold, wrap in foil without removing the lining paper.

Orange and Coffee Scones

INGREDIENTS

2¼ cups/225 g/8 oz plain (all-purpose) flour

½ tsp/2.5 g salt

2 tbsp/25 g/1 oz sugar

1 orange rind

4 tbsp/50 g/2 oz butter

2 tbsp/30 g instant coffee

⅔–1¼ cups/150 ml–275 ml/¼–½ pt buttermilk

12 sugar cubes

⅔ cup/150 ml/¼ pt orange juice

oven temperature 240°C/475°F/Gas 9

PREPARATION

☛ Mix together the flour, salt, sugar and orange rind and rub in the butter until the mixture resembles fine breadcrumbs.

☛ Dissolve the instant coffee in the buttermilk and bind the dough together.

☛ Roll out onto a floured board. Cut into scones and place on a floured baking tray.

☛ Dip the sugar cubes in the orange juice and press into the centre of each scone.

☛ Bake for 10–15 minutes and leave to cool.

☛ Serve warm, spread with butter.

Coffee and Apple Parcels

INGREDIENTS

SERVES 4

3½ cups/350 g/12 oz plain (all-purpose) flour

pinch of salt

⅓ cup/75 g/3 oz sugar

¾ cup/175 g/6 oz butter

2 eggs, beaten

FILLING

1 banana, mashed

2 rings pineapple, chopped finely

rind of one orange

4 apples

SAUCE

2 tbsp/25 g/1 oz butter

4 tbsp/25 g/1 oz plain (all-purpose) flour

⅔ cup/150 ml/¼ pt milk

¼ cup/50 ml/2 fl oz cooled extra strong coffee

⅔ cup/150 ml/¼ pt single (light) cream

oven temperature 220°C/425°F/Gas 7

PREPARATION

☛ Sift the flour, salt and ¼ cup/50 g/2 oz of sugar into a bowl. Rub in the butter until the mixture resembles fine breadcrumbs. Mix to a stiff pastry with the eggs.

☛ Mix together the bananas, pineapple, remaining sugar and orange rind.

☛ Peel and core the apples.

☛ Into a saucepan, put all the sauce ingredients, except the single cream, and heat, whisking all the time. When thick, remove from the heat and use a little of the sauce to moisten the fruit filling.

☛ Roll out the pastry to a square. Cut out four circles. Place an apple in the centre of each square and fill with the banana and pineapple mixture.

☛ Brush the edges with water and completely enclose the apple, pressing joins neatly together.

☛ Place the apple parcels, join side down, on a baking sheet and make a small hole in the centres. Decorate with pastry trimmings.

☛ Bake for 30 to 35 minutes on the centre shelf until golden.

☛ Gently heat the coffee sauce and add the single cream. Do not boil. Serve with the apples.

Coffee Fruit Loaf

INGREDIENTS

2¼ cups/225 g/8 oz strong (bread) flour
1 tsp/5 g salt
1 tsp/5 g sugar
small knob of lard
1 tbsp/15 g/½ oz fresh yeast
⅔ cup/150 ml/¼ pt tepid black coffee
¼ cup/50 g/2 oz vanilla sugar
⅓ cup/50 g/2 oz dried apricots, chopped
⅓ cup/50 g/2 oz dried figs, chopped
⅓ cup/50 g/2 oz roughly chopped almonds

TOPPING

2 tbsp/25 g/1 oz butter
6 tbsp/40 g/1½ oz plain (all purpose) flour
2 tbsp/25 g/1 oz vanilla sugar
1 tbsp/15 g instant coffee

oven temperature 200°C/400°F/Gas 6

PREPARATION

☞ Mix the flour, salt and sugar in a bowl and rub in the lard. Blend the yeast with the coffee and add to the flour, mixing to a soft dough that leaves the bowl clean. Cover with lightly greased polythene (plastic) and leave to rise in a warm place until doubled in size.

☞ Line and grease a 450 g/1 lb loaf pan. Gently knead in the sugar, apricots, figs and almonds, place in the prepared pan and cover with lightly oiled polythene. Leave to prove in a warm place until the mixture comes to the top of the pan.

☞ For the topping, rub the butter into the flour until the mixture resembles breadcrumbs. Stir in the sugar and coffee and spoon over the loaf. Bake for 40 to 45 minutes.

☞ Cool in the tin for 10 minutes and then turn out onto a wire rack.

☞ Serve sliced, spread with butter.

Coffee Almond Slice

INGREDIENTS

SERVES 10

SPONGE

½ cup/100 g/4 oz butter

½ cup/100 g/4 oz sugar

2 eggs

1 cup + 2 tbsp/100 g/4 oz self-raising (self-rising) flour

1 tbsp/15 g baking powder

⅓ cup/50 g/2 oz ground almonds

2 drops almond essence

1 tbsp/15 ml water

CREAM AND DECORATION

2 tbsp/25 g/1 oz plain chocolate

1¼ cups/275 ml/½ pt double (heavy) cream

4 tsp/20 g instant powdered coffee dissolved in 1 tbsp/15 ml hot water

3 tbsp/45 g icing (confectioner's) sugar

½ cup/50 g/2 oz chocolate vermicelli

oven temperature 180°C/350°F/Gas 4

PREPARATION

☞ Grease and line an 18 cm × 28 cm/7 in × 11 in pan with non-stick (waxed) paper.

☞ Put all the sponge ingredients in a bowl. Mix together and beat until smooth.

☞ Pour the batter into the prepared pan. Bake for 25 to 30 minutes until firm to the touch. Turn out, remove paper and cool.

☞ Melt the chocolate until runny and keep warm. Whisk the cream with the dissolved coffee and icing sugar until it forms soft peaks.

☞ Trim the edges of the cake and cut into three even-sized pieces.

☞ Spread a layer of cream on one piece, top with a second layer and spread with more cream. Top with the final layer of sponge cake.

☞ Spread the sides with cream and coat with the chocolate vermicelli. Spread the remaining cream on the top. Spoon the chocolate into a piping (pastry) bag with a fine nozzle. Pipe straight lines along the length of the cake and with the point of a knife draw lines backwards and forwards across the chocolate lines creating a chevron effect. Chill for at least 1 hour and serve.

Coffee Macaroons

INGREDIENTS

rice paper

⅔ cup/100 g/4 oz ground almonds

¾ cup/150 g/6 oz sugar

2 egg whites

1 tbsp/15 g cornflour (cornstarch)

¼ tsp/1.2 ml vanilla essence (extract)

1 tbsp/15 ml coffee essence

12 chocolate coffee beans

oven temperature 190°C/375°F/Gas 5

PREPARATION

☛ Line two or three baking trays with rice paper. Mix the ground almonds, sugar and all but one tbsp of the egg white together. Stir until all the ingredients are evenly blended. Stir in the cornflour, vanilla essence and coffee essence.

☛ Spoon into a piping (pastry) bag fitted with a 1.2 cm/½ in plain nozzle. Pipe the mixture onto the rice paper in large round circles. Top each one with a chocolate coffee bean. Brush with the remaining egg white.

☛ Bake the coffee macaroons for 15 minutes or until lightly browned, risen and slightly cracked.

☛ Cut the rice paper to fit round each coffee macaroon and leave to cool on a wire rack.

Coffee Knots

INGREDIENTS

SERVES 8–10

1 tbsp/15 g/½ oz fresh yeast

4 tbsp/60 ml tepid strong milky coffee

1 tsp/5 g vanilla sugar

2¼ cups/225 g/8 oz strong white (bread) flour

½ tsp/2.5 ml salt

2 tbsp/25 g/1 oz butter

1 egg, beaten

vegetable oil for deep frying

1 tsp/5 g sugar

1 tsp/5 g cocoa

PREPARATION

☛ Blend the yeast with the coffee and sugar. Leave in a warm place until frothy.

☛ Sift the flour and salt into a large bowl and rub in the butter. Add the egg and yeast liquid to the dry ingredients and beat for five minutes.

☛ Divide the dough into eight to ten pieces and shape into an 18 cm/7 in long roll. Tie each into a knot.

☛ Heat the oil to 180°C/350°F and fry the doughnuts for 5 to 10 minutes, until golden brown.

☛ Drain on kitchen (paper) towels. Stir sugar and cocoa together and toss the warm doughnuts in it.

Sweetheart Cookies

INGREDIENTS

SERVES 10–12

½ cup/100 g/4 oz butter

½ cup/100 g/4 oz sugar

2 tbsp/30 ml coffee essence

1 egg

2¾ cups/275 g/10 oz plain (all-purpose) flour

DECORATION

¾ cup/100 g/4 oz icing (confectioner's) sugar, sieved

1–2 tbsp/15–30 ml warm water

a few drops of red food colouring

pink and cream ribbons 12 mm/½ in wide

oven temperature 180°C/350°F/Gas 4

PREPARATION

☞ Cream the butter and sugar together until pale and fluffy. Stir in the coffee essence and egg, and mix thoroughly.

☞ Fold in the flour and turn the mixture onto a board dusted with icing sugar.

☞ Knead gently and roll out to 6 mm/¼ in thickness and cut into heart shapes. Cut a smaller heart shape in the centre for the ribbon.

☞ Place on a baking tray and bake for approximately 15 minutes and leave to cool.

☞ Put the decoration ingredients into a bowl and mix until smooth. Spoon into a piping (pastry) bag with a fine plain nozzle and pipe around the edges of the cookies and round the shape in the centre.

☞ Allow to dry and thread the ribbons through the cookies and tie.

Coffee Orange Soufflés

INGREDIENTS

SERVES 6

6 large thick-skinned oranges

3 eggs, separated

½ cup/100 g/4 oz sugar

1 tbsp/15 g powdered instant coffee

2 tbsp/30 g cornflour (cornstarch)

1 tbsp/15 ml Cointreau

oven temperature 220°C/425°F/Gas 7

PREPARATION

☛ With a sharp knife, cut the top from each orange and a thin slice from the base so that the oranges stand upright.

☛ Using a teaspoon or grapefruit knife, gently remove the flesh from the inside. Squeeze the flesh to extract the juice and strain it.

☛ Beat together the egg yolks, sugar, coffee and cornflour. Dilute with the orange juice. Place over a low heat and, stirring constantly, bring to the boil. When thickened, remove from the heat and stir in the orange liqueur. Cover and leave to cool.

☛ Thirty minutes before serving, whisk the egg whites until they form really stiff peaks and gently fold into the coffee cream.

☛ Spoon the filling into the shells until level.

☛ Transfer to an ovenproof dish and bake for 10 to 15 minutes or until well risen and set.

☛ Serve immediately.

Individual Coffee Fruit Flans

INGREDIENTS

SERVES 8

SPONGE CASES

½ cup/100 g/4 oz butter

½ cup/100 g/4 oz vanilla sugar

2 eggs

grated rind of one lemon

1 cup + 2 tbsp/100 g/4 oz self-raising (self-rising) flour

1 tsp/5 g baking powder

1 tbsp/15 g instant coffee powder

FILLING

1½–2 cups/225 g/8 oz selection of fruits eg peaches, apricots, green grapes, strawberries, etc.

GLAZE

2 tbsp/15 g/½ oz powdered gelatine (gelatin)

⅔ cup/150 ml/¼ pt orange juice

oven temperature 190°C/375°F/Gas 5

PREPARATION

☛ Cream the butter and vanilla sugar together until light and fluffy. Gradually beat in the eggs and lemon rind. Sift together the flour, baking powder and instant coffee and gently fold into the cream mixture with a metal spoon.

☛ Grease eight individual muffin or cupcake pans and divide the mixture between them.

☛ Bake for 15 minutes until cooked through.

☛ Remove from the tins and cool on a wire rack.

☛ Slice or halve fruit, as required. Fill the sponge cases making little domes of the fruit.

☛ Melt the gelatine in two tablespoons of juice and add the remaining liquid.

☛ Cool until just on the point of setting.

☛ Spoon over the fruit in the sponge cases and leave to set.

NB For a more extravagant version of this dessert, soak the cases with your favourite liqueur and serve with sweetened whipped cream.

Sweets

Opposite: Coffee Mallows (*see page 116.*)

Coffee Mallows

INGREDIENTS

2 cups/450 g/1 lb sugar

2 tbsp/25 g/1 oz golden (corn) syrup

2/3 cup/150 ml/1/4 pt water

2 tbsp/30 g powdered gelatine (gelatin)

2/3 cup/150 ml/1/4 pt strong Italian coffee

2 egg whites

vanilla essence (extract)

icing (confectioner's) sugar

cornflour (cornstarch)

PREPARATION

☛ Slowly dissolve sugar, syrup and water in a large, heavy-based pan. Bring to the boil. While the mixture is boiling, dissolve the gelatine in the coffee.

☛ Remove the syrup from the heat and slowly add the gelatine, stirring well.

☛ Whisk the egg whites until just foaming and pour onto the hot syrup in a thin stream, whisking all the time.

☛ Add a few drops of vanilla essence and continue whisking until the mixture is thick and stiff.

☛ Pour into a 25 cm/9 in square loose-bottom cake pan, lined with greased (waxed) non-stick paper.

☛ Leave uncovered overnight and check that the coffee mallow is completely set before removing from the pan and cutting into squares.

☛ Roll each piece thoroughly in a mixture of one part cornflour and two parts icing sugar.

☛ You can cut the coffee mallow into rounds using biscuit (cookie) cutters. Dip the cutter into the cornflour and icing sugar mixture between cuts to prevent the cutter from sticking.

Coffee Truffles

INGREDIENTS

MAKES 18–24

½ cup/100 g/4 oz plain chocolate

4 tbsp/50 g/2 oz butter

¾ cup/100 g/4 oz icing (confectioner's) sugar

2 cups/100 g/4 oz coffee cake, crumbled

1 egg yolk

1 tsp/5 ml Crême de Cacao

chocolate vermicelli

PREPARATION

☛ Melt the chocolate and butter in a bowl over a saucepan of hot water.

☛ Remove from heat and stir in remaining ingredients except the chocolate vermicelli.

☛ Chill in the refrigerator until firm enough to handle. Mould into balls the size of a small walnut and roll in the vermicelli.

☛ Leave to set on greaseproof (waxed) paper before placing in individual paper cases (paper cups).

Java Jam

MAKES 1KG/2LB

450 g/1 lb bananas, sliced

2½ cups/550 ml/1 pt orange juice

2½ cups/550 ml/1 pt sweetened black coffee

1¼ cups/275 g/10 oz rich brown soft sugar

¼ cup/50 g/2 oz vanilla sugar

PREPARATION

☛ Put all ingredients into a pan and bring to the boil. Reduce the heat and cook gently until the mixture softens and becomes thick.
☛ Stir frequently to prevent burning on the bottom of the pan. Spoon into sterilized jars.

Coconut Ice

INGREDIENTS

MAKES 18—24

2 cups/450 g/1 lb granulated sugar

⅔ cup/150 ml/¼ pt milk

1½ cups/150 g/5 oz desiccated (shredded) coconut

2 tbsp/30 ml coffee essence.

PREPARATION

☛ Put the sugar and milk into a large heavy-based saucepan and gently heat until the sugar has dissolved.

☛ Boil for 10 to 15 minutes. The mixture should form a soft ball when a little is dropped in cold water.

☛ Remove from the heat and stir in the coconut. Pour half the mixture into a greased 15 cm/6 in loose-bottom square cake pan.

☛ Quickly add the coffee essence to the remaining mixture and pour into the cake pan.

☛ Smooth the top and mark into squares or bars when half set.

☛ Remove from the pan when cold and set.

Coffee Mint Crystals

INGREDIENTS

MAKES 550G/1¼LB

2 cups/450 g/1 lb sugar

¾ cup/100 g/4 oz powdered glucose

⅔ cup/150 ml/¼ pt water

1¾ cups/175 g/6 oz desiccated (shredded) coconut

2 tbsp/30 ml coffee essence

4 tbsp/25 g/1 oz mint chocolate, coarsely grated

PREPARATION

☛ In a large heavy-based pan, put the sugar, glucose and water, and bring to the boil.

☛ Remove from heat and stir in the coconut, coffee essence and mint chocolate.

☛ Spoon into small rocky heaps on waxed paper and leave to set.

☛ Serve in small paper cases (paper cups).

Mocha Cups

INGREDIENTS

MAKES 18–20

½ cup/100 g/4 oz milk chocolate

½ cup + 2 tbsp/150 g/5 oz plain chocolate

4 tbsp/60 ml strong Italian coffee

4 tbsp/50 g/2 oz butter, softened

2 egg yolks

rum to taste

slivers of burnt almonds

PREPARATION

☛ Melt the milk chocolate in a bowl over hot water until liquid. Pour a teaspoon of chocolate inside the paper sweet cases (candy paper) and run it round the inside to line the case completely. Leave to set.

☛ Remove the paper cases from the chocolate cups. Melt the plain chocolate and stir in the coffee. Leave to cool.

☛ Beat in the butter and egg yolks. Add rum to taste.

☛ Pipe or spoon the mocha filling into the chocolate cups and decorate with the almond slivers.

Superior Prunes

INGREDIENTS

2 cups/450 g/1 lb Demerara sugar

½ cup/100 ml/4 fl oz cold coffee

2¼ cups/450 g/1 lb prunes, stoned

1¾ cups/400 ml/¾ pt Kahlua or Crême de Cacao

½ cup/100 ml/4 fl oz vodka

PREPARATION

☛ Put the sugar and coffee into a medium heavy-based pan. Bring to the boil stirring all the time. Reduce heat and simmer for 5 minutes.

☛ Add the prunes and simmer gently for a further 40 minutes. Remove the prunes with a slotted spoon and put into sterilized jars.

☛ Mix together the Kahlua or Crême de Cacao and vodka and half fill the jars. Cover with the syrup and seal the jars.

Coffee Creams

INGREDIENTS

MAKES 24

1 egg, separated

3⅓ cups/450 g/1 lb icing (confectioner's) sugar

2 tbsp/30 ml coffee essence, or extra strong instant coffee

PREPARATION

☞ Beat the egg white until frothy but not stiff. Sift the icing sugar into a bowl and mix with enough of the egg white to make a firm paste.

☞ Add the coffee essence, mix and knead together. Roll out on a board well dusted with icing sugar and cut into small circles.

☞ Place on waxed paper and leave overnight until set and firm to the touch.

Coffee Nougat

INGREDIENTS

MAKES 675G/1½LB

¾ cup/100 g/4 oz whole hazelnuts, browned

½ cup/50 g/2 oz candied orange rind

½ cup/50 g/2 oz glacé (candied) cherries of different colours

2 cups/450 g/1 lb sugar

1⅔ cups/225 g/8 oz powdered glucose

⅔ cup/150 ml/¼ pt water

2 egg whites

2 tbsp/30 ml coffee essence

rice paper

PREPARATION

☞ Roughly chop the hazelnuts, candied orange rind and glacé cherries. In a large heavy-based pan, heat the sugar, glucose and water gently until the sugar dissolves and then boil. Whisk the egg whites in a bowl until stiff and gradually add the syrup. Keep beating until the mixture thickens. This could take up to 30 minutes but it is important if the nougat is going to set.

☞ Add the coffee essence, nuts, candied orange and cherries, and mix well.

☞ Pour into an 18 cm/7 in square cake pan lined with rice paper. Cover with another sheet of rice paper and press down with a weight.

☞ Leave for 12 hours. Remove from pan and cut into squares.

Coffee Fudge

INGREDIENTS

MAKES 18—24

1 cup/225 g/8 oz butter

4 cups/900 g/2 lb granulated sugar

2 cups/450 ml/16 oz evaporated milk

½ cup/100 ml/4 fl oz water

½ cup/100 ml/4 fl oz strong coffee

⅓ cup/50 g/2 oz seeded raisins, chopped

PREPARATION

☛ Place all the ingredients, except the raisins, into a large heavy-based pan. Stir gently over a low heat until the sugar is dissolved.

☛ Bring to the boil and maintain, stirring occasionally, until a teaspoon of fudge dropped into half a cup of cold water will form a soft ball.

☛ Remove from heat, dip the base of the pan into cold water and leave for 5 minutes. Beat with a wooden spoon until the mixture loses its gloss, looks grainy, thickens a little and will just pour from the pan.

☛ Quickly stir in the raisins and pour into a greased pan 30 cm × 15 cm/12 in × 7 in. Leave until cold and set, and cut into squares.

☛ Wrap in waxed paper.